Being Scottish in Italy

Being Scottish in Italy

(Or…I'll give it two years)

Fraser Lauchlan

Copyright © 2018 Fraser Lauchlan

All rights reserved.

ISBN:
ISBN-13: 9781790443413

DEDICATION

To John (Iain) Milne Lauchlan (3.7.1943 -- 3.11.2013)

If you find any of the contents of this book funny, then it's because of him. He taught me everything I know about trying to be funny. As well as many other things.

CONTENTS

Prologue 1
1. Origini 3
2. Il trasferimento 8
3. La lingua italiana 13
4. Il concorso 18
5. La burocrazia 25
6. Religione 31
7. Cappuccino 38
8. Calcio 46
9. Trasporti 53
10. Il clima 61
11. Buon lavoro! 71
12. Zanzare 79
13. Cibo 86
14. Bambini 95
15. Il presepe 105
16. Tradizioni 113
17. The verde verde grass of home 122
18. Graffiti 133

19. Carnevale 142

20. Papà, pappa e il papa 151

21. Baci 164

22. Montalbano sono 172

23. Pasquetta 182

24. La strada nuova 192

25. Sagra 203

26. La prima comunione.................................. 212

27. Controlli 224

28. Birra, pizza e caffè..................................... 233

29. Salute! 242

30. Festa! 251

31. Raccomandazioni 260

32. Being scozzese in Italy............................... 274

Epilogue 282

ACKNOWLEDGMENTS

There are so many people I'd like to thank that have helped me with the preparation of this book, mostly family and close friends, but also others who have helped me in some shape or form along the way. The following may have given me feedback on earlier drafts of this book, or have given me encouragement by commenting positively on individual chapters that were originally published as blogs. Some people have also contributed directly to some of the ideas contained therein. Some of the following people have also appeared in the book, although most names have been changed for the purposes of privacy and/or anonymity. In no particular order, I'd like to thank the following as without you, this book would not have happened: Serena Meloni, Nana Lauchlan, Dougie Lauchlan, Costantino Usai, Sonia Meloni, Rosetta Bernardo, Efisio Meloni, Derek Cooper, Norma Cooper, David McCubbin, Graham Christie, Phil Stringer, Brendan Lawlor, Patrick Tinley, Christy Kennedy, Antonio Fregola, Marta Kadziela, Anna Salis, Janette Black, Alan Black, Marco Hessels, Angela Quinn (who gave me the idea of the different kinds of car horn use during a visit to Sardinia), Eleanor Hamilton, Dorothy Hill, Ronnie Hill, Ian King (do these railings lead to my hotel?), Jim Boyle, Angela Stewart, Annie Smith, Caroline Spinks, Polly Jones, Julie Kiddie, Rhona Larney, Adele Humphries, Clare Daly, Mhari Greenwood, Esra McCabe, Elisa Jones, Martha Ramsay, Paula Dudgeon, David Dunsmore, Gordon Harrow, Gearoid Loughnane, Valentina Simeone, Lorna Attia, Anna Nolan, Ana de Mentaberry, Colin Thomson, Shiona Thomson, John Thomson, Emma Happell, Paul McGill, Maurizio Atzeni, Valeria Atzeni, Maria Carme Parafita Couto, Lindsay Clayton, Alessio Saba, Simona Lecce, Laura Serra, Alessio Trois, Rachel Cole, Denise Bates, Anne Clare Brown, Rossella Locci, Neil Farquharson, Margaret Mary Moran, Bernie Moran, Valeria Carrucciu, Monia Piroddi, Giada Piroddi, Giorgio Mulas, Giorgio Piroddi, Daniela Ligas (senior), Daniela Ligas (junior) (who provided me with the information about traditional Sardinian costumes), Gianfranco Meloni, Sandra Zago, Anna Puggioni, Giacomo Ligas, Enrica Busalla, Ottavio Atzeni, Anna Rita Spiga, Michela Atzeni, and Angela Serra.

Last, but not least, a huge thanks to the

wonderful Maria Tedde who created the fantastic book cover and the map of Sardinia.

Thank you, everyone!

Map of Sardinia

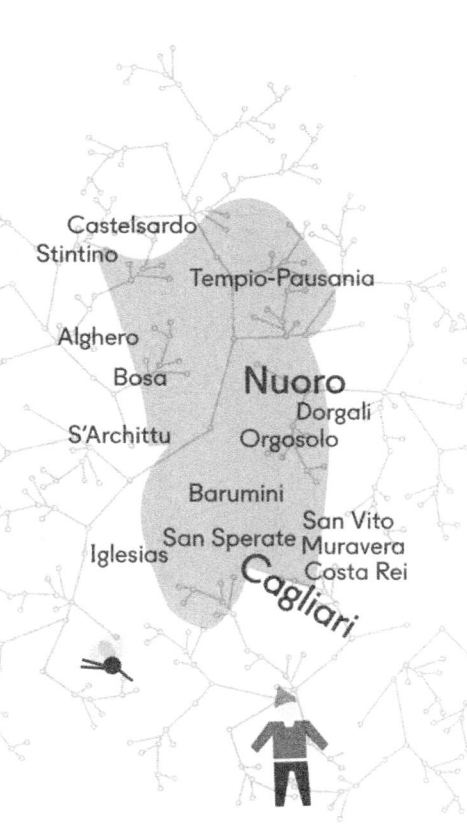

Castelsardo
Stintino
Tempio-Pausania
Alghero
Bosa
Nuoro
Dorgali
S'Archittu
Orgosolo
Barumini
San Vito
Iglesias San Sperate Muravera
Costa Rei
Cagliari

Prologue

Moving abroad at any age can bring its own challenges as well as its own elements of excitement. Especially if one is moving to a language and culture that is so different from your own. At the age of 36, after living almost all of my life in Scotland, I was suddenly propelled into exactly this kind of scenario.

After having coped with the Scottish climate for more than 10 years, my Italian wife had decided that she had had enough and wanted to move back home. Home was Sardinia, the Italian island in the middle of the Mediterranean Sea. Just a few weeks after we moved, I recall vividly the sight of the huge articulated transporter driving down the street of our newly-rented house. Inside were all our valued possessions that had travelled all the way from Edinburgh – 1600 miles and two ferry journeys. I thought to myself, *"there's no going back now, Fraser"*. At least not in the short term.

I could still remember the words of my boss and mentor, Jim, who had always given me sage advice over the 20 years I had known him, *"you've got to give it 2 years, Fraser. At least 2 years. And then decide whether you like it or not"*. He told me the story of his cousin, Jean, who moved with her husband to Canada when she was in her mid-30s. Unsure about emigrating abroad, she had told Jim that she would stay about two years, after which she would return to Scotland. Forty years later, she was still there. I had promised myself to heed Jim's advice. Give it 2 years and then see.

After we moved, I started to note down some observations of my new life. Things that happened, conversations that took place. I found it all fascinating. Good things, bad things, funny things, sad things. This book is largely based on the events of those first two years when I was trying to cope with *Being Scottish in Italy*.

CHAPTER ONE

Origini

Everybody loves Italy. Ok, maybe not everyone, but a lot of people do. Including me. I feel as if I've always loved Italy - and all things Italian - but when I think back to my childhood and adolescence, I can certainly pinpoint three reasons why I began this love affair with *il bel paese*.

The first reason dates back to 1982, when the football World Cup was being played in Spain. I was 10 years old at the time. Remarkably, Scotland actually qualified for this one (indeed, it was during the time when we *always* qualified for World Cups: seems like a century ago now). Initially I had taken a little shine to the Brazilian team at that World Cup: they played with a swagger and a confidence that I hadn't ever seen before, with players like Zico, Socrates, Falcao, Junior, to name but a few. I liked them despite the fact they stuffed Scotland 4-1 in the group stages.

Brazil went on to qualify for the next stages. However, they met their match in the Quarter Finals against Italy in a thrilling encounter, sometimes referred to as the greatest World Cup match ever. Italy won 3-2, with a hat-trick from Paolo Rossi, and I still have vivid memories of watching that game. It is probably the finest game I have ever witnessed in all the years that I have been following football. As a result, my support quickly switched to the Italians. Italy went on and won the World Cup final against West Germany 3-1 at the Bernabéu Stadium in Madrid on the 11th July 1982. With their bright azure blue tops (I learned many years afterwards that the Italian team were known as the *Azzurri* on account of their shirts) and dazzling white shorts, I watched them humiliate a strong West German team with many household names such as Rumminigge, Breitner and Littbarksi.

Everyone who watched that game will remember the iconic image of Marco Tardelli scoring the 2nd and decisive goal, running from one end of the pitch to the other, with mouth wide open, wild blazing eyes, burning with the satisfaction of having just achieved something great, his arms stretched out wide waving like an aeroplane in tune to his head nodding from side to side. It's an image that I copied all summer when I scored a tap-in down the park when playing with my friends. For me, Marco Tardelli's run summed up the passion, the vivacity, the *joie de vivre* that I loved about the Italians. I was hooked from that day on.

I grew up in Kilmarnock, a small town in the south-west of Scotland. There weren't loads of Italians around when I was growing up, but there were some, mostly running ice-cream parlours, greengrocers or fish and chip shops. One of my favourite places growing up was Varani's, known as The Forum, which was an ice-cream parlour, and is still going to this day. It's a Kilmarnock institution. Everyone who lives in Kilmarnock - and probably those in the neighbouring towns and villages as well - know about the Forum ice-cream. It serves what many regard as the best vanilla ice-cream in the land.

The Forum, and these other few shops dotted around Kilmarnock, were run by the Italian families of the town: it was often the case that all the relatives would work in these shops. I used to go into one of these shops every day to buy my 10p bag of penny sweets, a Texan bar, a packet of Spangles, or something else that probably no longer exists. I deliberately went into this shop, not because it was close to my home, or because it was on the road back from school, but because the girl serving at the till was the most beautiful girl I had ever seen. Francesca had long, dark, curly hair, a colour of skin rarely seen in the cold and wet climes of south-west Scotland (this was the 1980s before the proliferation of sun beds, but anyway, this was a natural, authentic darker colour to the skin, not like some battered leather). She had big, beautiful brown eyes, and an amazing figure. I loved her. She was way out of my league (she was 3 years older than me for a start), and indeed the love was never reciprocated. This was the second reason why I fell in love with Italy, or more precisely an Italian. And, even though the love was never reciprocated, it just increased my fascination and slow-burning obsession with all things Italian.

The third reason why I fell in love happened around the same time. It was 1985. I went to see a film at the cinema. It wasn't *Ghostbusters*, or *Back to the Future*. It was called *A Room with a View*. The film adaptation of E.M. Forster's novel, starring Daniel Day Lewis and Helena Bonham-Carter. The film (and book) is mainly set in Tuscany, and in particular, the city of Florence and the Tuscan countryside. I absolutely loved this film. I fell in love with Florence, and everything else about the ambience of the film (and maybe Helena Bonham-Carter had a little influence on me too, if I'm honest). I knew I had to visit this place.

Fast forward 10 years or so, when I was in my early 20s. I was studying at University down in England, and I happened to latch onto a group of Italian exchange students, who were visiting from

Cagliari, the capital of Sardinia. I started to date one of them, Stefania. She was even better than Francesca or Helena Bonham-Carter. She was the real thing. She had long, dark curly hair, beautiful eyes and was beautiful everywhere else. Finally, I fell in love for the fourth time with something (or, I should say, someone) Italian.

Stefania and I have been together ever since. I'm Scottish. She's Italian. It was a good cultural mix. Or so we thought. This is what this book is all about. We moved to Italy after almost 10 years of marriage and living in Edinburgh. Stefania was desperate to move back home, mainly because she was fed up with the Scottish climate after putting up with it for so long. But she also wanted to be closer to her family after our children were born.

When we moved to Italy, it was truly an eye-opening experience for me. I had visited several times before we moved: for summer holidays, Christmases, Easters and so on. But living over here was something else. I started to notice things about living in Italy that are so different, and I mean **so different**, from my upbringing in the west coast of Scotland. But before we get to that, I need to rewind a bit. There's a bit of a story to tell before we even left Scottish soil.

CHAPTER TWO

Il trasferimento

The move - *il trasferimento* - back to Italy was not an easy one. It took us more than 2 years to complete the move from the point where we had decided that's what we wanted to do. Stefania and I had already been married for several years, and had been a couple for almost 10 years (from the time when she had first come to the UK as a student). We were living in Edinburgh with our two young children, Luca and Anna. Stefania had been living in Scotland pretty much ever since we met.

Anyway, it was a fairly ordinary morning one

day in November when I left our home in Edinburgh to go to work. I hadn't noticed anything particularly different about her mood, or had picked up on anything she had said (I'm a psychologist by the way - cough cough - no, really, I am). Nevertheless, while at work later that day I received a text message on my mobile phone while in the middle of a meeting …

"I'VE HAD ENOUGH. I WANT TO GO BACK HOME".

The problem with modern technology is that you cannot always 'read' accurately into the meaning of people's communications. My immediate response was:

"Where is she? Is she not at home at the moment? What's happened?",

followed by the slow realisation that to Stefania, even after 10 years, home meant Italy. This thought was quickly followed further by the doubt in my mind:

"Does she mean to include me in these plans to go back 'home'?"

I suppose it's not the ideal means to be informed that a major life-changing event is going to happen in your life, but there you are. That's how I found out. After we put the kids to bed that night (Luca was nearly 3 years old at that time, and Anna, our daughter, was only 4 months), we finally had the chance to talk. And I had the chance to ask some questions. I felt it would be prudent to start off with probably the most important question:

"Am I included in these plans?",

quickly followed by:

"Did you mean you've had enough of me?"

I felt these were reasonable questions to ask. After all, we'd had our ups and downs, like any couple, but by and large we did get on ok, even if the previous few months had been difficult since our daughter was born, leaving precious little time for us as a couple. Inevitably this led to more arguments than maybe we were used to, but nothing, I felt anyway, that we couldn't overcome.

I needn't have worried. Stefania laughed off my questions, brushing them aside:

"Of course it includes you, ye eejit" (Stefania had picked up on some fine Scottish words in her time over there).

I would like to think that the major influencing factor in her "inviting" me along was that my wife was still in love with me after all these years and found my charm and engaging personality irresistible. However, maybe I should also have considered some of the statistics involved. Italy has one of the lowest divorce rates in Western Europe (only Portugal has a lower rate - and both are considerably lower than the UK), and while I would have preferred to have thought otherwise, maybe this cultural aspect bore some of the influence involved in my wife's decision making. The truth was maybe somewhere in-between.

Luckily for me, Stefania's wish to return home did have certain advantages. Sardinia, the Italian island slap bang in the middle of the Mediterranean, was considered Italy's jewel in the crown: amazing, award-winning beaches, a fantastic climate and a consequent lifestyle more in keeping with the relaxed way of life that I had always envied. I was starting to get excited.

"When can we go? Will I start packing my bags?"

Stefania quickly crushed my excitement.

"We can't go yet. We'll need to find work. How are we going to support a young family if we've no income to rely on?"

She did have a point of course. I was just getting carried away too quickly by the idea of moving to sunnier climes. It was November in Scotland after all. What I hadn't perhaps considered though, was how long it would take for one of us to find work in Sardinia.

Let me explain something here. Italy is very much a divided country, in many ways, but probably the single most significant difference one finds in Italy is the difference between the North (that is, everywhere north of Rome) and the South (from Rome 'downwards'). Climatically, culturally, and more importantly for our possible move, economically, Sardinia is considered part of the South of Italy (though I do have to qualify this by stating that many in Sardinia, mainly separatists, would disagree and claim that Sardinia stands alone from this dichotomy).

What does this mean? Put simply, it means that there is less money in the South, less jobs, less prospects and more financial hardship all round. I do remember one of our visits to the South of Italy, in the region of Calabria located in the 'toe' of the boot of Italy, and some of the poverty we witnessed was difficult to fathom, especially when one considers that Italy is a Western European, 'first' world country. The contrast with the rich, fertile North is striking. Anyway, while Sardinia perhaps did not have the same austerity of some of the living conditions that we witnessed in Calabria, nevertheless, there were little job prospects out there. We had to be patient.

CHAPTER THREE

La lingua italiana

When the dust settled after that initial life-changing day in November, I did begin to have some doubts about the move. When Stefania and I first met all those years ago while at University, and when we both began to realise that we were becoming involved in a committed relationship, we had to discuss how this was going to work. I was Scottish, she was Italian. At that time, my life was in the UK, I was in the middle of my post-graduate studies at University, meanwhile Stefania was still to finish off her undergraduate degree in Italy (she had only visited the UK for an exchange visit). Stefania said she was willing to move to Scotland after completing her studies. In return, I said that if she were willing to make such a move, then it was only fair that I reciprocate the gesture: if, at any time, she wanted to go back home, then I would be willing to make a go of things over in Sardinia. It seemed the natural thing for me to do: how else can a committed relationship work? I didn't realise how long it would take before that promise was asked to be fulfilled.

There was one major difference, however, since I had made that promise 10 years previously. We now had children, and therefore the promise to move was, all things considered, a much bigger and more significant one than the one made as a 24-year-old post-graduate student. I had my family to consider here as well, not only for the impact that the move would have on my children's relationships with their grandparents, aunts, uncles, cousins, and so on, but there was something altogether much more important than this in my eyes. My children would be brought up as Italian with a Scottish father, not as Scottish with an Italian mother. I perhaps hadn't fully considered this before now.

Please don't misunderstand me: I was not against the idea of my children being brought up as Italian, far from it. As I've explained already in the first chapter, I had always had a love of things Italian, ever since I was 10 years old. There was something about Italy and Italians that had always captured my attention. And when I met Stefania at

University, I was able to develop this admiring and affectionate relationship with Italy in a much more substantial and significant manner, including learning the language (*la lingua italiana*).

After 6 months of being together when she was on an exchange visit, Stefania had to return to Italy for a short while to complete her studies. It was at that point that we made our pact of being open to living in each other's country. I hadn't ever visited Italy at this point in my life, though a few months after Stefania returned to Sardinia, just after Christmas time, I put this right. Before visiting for the first time I had made a special effort to learn some Italian. There was a particular reason for this, over and above the fact that I had always wanted to learn the language, as it had always struck me as such a beautiful language (I'm trying my best here not to sound like John Gordon Sinclair from Gregory's Girl, but somehow I still manage it ... Gregory: *"it's such a beautiful language. Don't you think it's ... so alive?"* Italian teacher: *"And what have you learned then Gregory?"* Gregory: *"Oh, just a couple of words ... eh Bella and ... eh ... Bella"*).

Anyway, there was another source of motivation for me to learn Italian. It is now a legendary story within our family that Stefania's father was, let's say, far from pleased, when his daughter rang up from the UK to say that she had met someone important while studying over there, and that she was hoping to introduce him to her family sometime soon.

There is something particularly significant and noteworthy in this statement. Introducing a boyfriend or girlfriend to your family in Italy, certainly in the culture of Southern Italy, sends a very strong message. It is statement of intent, going beyond the mere presentation of a boyfriend or girlfriend as it is in British culture. By introducing your boyfriend, you are no longer a *"ragazzo"* but a *"fidanzato"*. I don't think I need to translate the significance of the latter word but let's just say that without me realising it, I was going to be projected into an environment where there was an expectation on me to marry, if not sooner, then certainly later. This was despite the fact that there was never any marriage proposal or serious discussion about it between us.

Thus, to get back to the story, the alternative source of my motivation to learn Italian arose from Stefania's father's reaction to his daughter's communication that she had met someone with whom it was likely she was going to be involved in a long-term relationship. Family legend now has it that he turned to his wife, now my mother-in-law and said *"Ma che scherzo è? Quindi, invece di parlare al mio genero, sarà sempre meglio parlare a quella sedia."* This roughly translates as: "Is this some kind of joke? For a son-in-law I might as well just have that chair, as I might be able to talk to it more".

I had to show him. I *could* learn his language. I *could* talk just as much as that chair.

I studied Italian every night for at least 30 minutes for 3 months solid. Every night, seven days a week, for 3 months. Eventually things started to seep through. It was the best thing I could ever have done. While I could not claim for a second that I was fully fluent on that first visit, it certainly gave me a solid foundation on which I was able to build on each subsequent visit. After a couple more visits to see Stefania I did get to the point where I could confidently state that I was fluent in Italian: a dream for me, and also the envy of many of my friends back home, who like me had struggled to grasp the basics of French or German at secondary school, mainly because of how late in our school careers it was taught (from first year of secondary school: 12 years old), and the mode of teaching to which we were exposed (yep, nothing to do with our complete ineptitude at learning languages).

Perhaps more importantly, however, Stefania's father was impressed. I still remember the "meeting" we had in the kitchen at the end of my first visit. He took me aside to let me know that he thought I was a *"bravo ragazzo"* and that he was struck by how much Italian I could speak. I had done it. I had won him over. Not an easy task it has to be said, but I managed it. I had cleared the path for us to think about a more formal commitment. Three years later we were married.

CHAPTER FOUR

Il concorso

I've already said how difficult it would be to find work in Sardinia, and how patient Stefania had warned me to be after her initial communication that she wanted to move back home after 10 years in Scotland. What I hadn't realised was how long, painful and drawn-out the process would be. For any Italians reading this, or anyone who has some knowledge of Italy, you may be surprised to hear that I'm going to attempt to explain what a public *"concorso"* is. On first sight, it seems such an inoffensive word, but the truth is, it symbolises for Italians, and anyone else who has ever applied for a public-sector job in Italy, a painful, stressful, potentially heart-breaking experience that will consume your life for at least 18 months, and possibly even more.

Growing up in Scotland, I always thought that the selection procedure regarding public sector jobs, just like most other jobs, was fairly straightforward:

1. you apply for a job by completing an application form,
2. if you're fortunate, you are short-listed for an interview a short time later
3. if you perform well at the interview you may be offered the job
4. If you do not perform well enough, you are informed of such and you know there may be other opportunities on the horizon soon afterwards. You may even be given feedback by those who interviewed you, in order to help you to improve your interview technique for that next opportunity.

In Italy, it does not quite work like this. My God, I wish it did. It would have saved me from much stress, anxiety and I would probably still have a full head of hair. To give you a rough idea of how a "*concorso*" works (which translates generally as "competition" but in this particular context my Collins Italian-English dictionary translates it as "work related competitive exam"), I'll describe precisely what Stefania had to go through in order to (thankfully) be successful in 'winning' a public-sector job working for the Sardinian Regional Government:

1. apply for the job by completing an application form,
2. fly over from Edinburgh to Sardinia to sit a multiple-choice exam on the subject of epidemiology and bio-statistics (for which you will have studied endlessly while trying to hold down your current job and caring after your two young children) along with the other 150 candidates, taking your 10-month-old daughter with you, as you are still breast-feeding
3. Wait several weeks before being informed that you have done well enough on the multiple-choice exam. You have 'passed' to the next stage. You now have to study endlessly again for the next instalment: a written exam, which will take place in the following 3-6 months (date to be decided).
4. Five months later fly over from Edinburgh to Sardinia to sit a written exam along with 25 other successful candidates, again with

your young daughter, leaving your husband and 3-year-old son in Edinburgh.
5. Wait several weeks before being informed that you have done well enough to proceed to the next stage: an oral exam. Again, precise date and location to be decided in the next 3-6 months (Note: I have made the mistake in the past of describing this as Stefania finally making it to the interview stage. As I have been frequently told: it is not an interview, it is an oral exam). Again, you have to study intensively for this stage of the *"concorso"*, while trying to hold down your own job in Scotland and help care for your two young children (Another note: the truth, of course, was that the familial responsibilities fell on *my* shoulders while Stefania was studying, on top of trying to keep my own job going at the same time ... surely this is worthy of some kind of formal recognition).
6. Fly over again from Edinburgh to Sardinia for a third time for the oral exam, along with four other candidates.

7. Wait several more weeks before being told that your performance on all of the exams has been taken into account and that you completed the "*concorso*" as 3rd out of all the 150 candidates or so that had applied. Unfortunately, this means that you cannot be offered a job just now, but you will be placed on a waiting list with the other four candidates who made it to the oral exam stage of the "*concorso*". This waiting list will expire in 18 months and, if the necessary funds are made available within that time, you will be called and offered a job.
8. Wait a year (yes, you read correctly: a YEAR) and you receive a phone call to say that the Minister for Health for the Sardinian Regional Government would like to have a meeting with you. You have a meeting with said person (luckily you just happen to be in Sardinia at the time on holiday, or otherwise, this would have involved another flight from Edinburgh to Sardinia) where it seems clear that you are soon going to be called for a job, although there is no explicit mention

of the offer of a job during this meeting.
9. Wait 3 more months until, finally, there is a letter delivered to your parents' address in Sardinia, offering you a full-time, fixed post working for the Sardinian Regional Government as a "funzionario: esperto in epidimologia e bio-statistica" (translation: something to do with Public Health).

As you can see, the process is a bit more complicated and drawn-out than how we operate in the UK, and, while I do admit that some of the details above are specific to our situation, nonetheless, it does represent a fairly accurate picture of what someone endures when applying for a full-time public-sector job in Italy. I was becoming increasingly frustrated as the process went on, though I was trying my best to be supportive. However, between stages 8 and 9, my patience and understanding were being tested to their absolute limits. I nearly lost it. I just could not comprehend how, after sitting several exams, seemingly doing well, even meeting with the highest officer in the organisation where Stefania had applied to work, we were still no clearer about the possibility of Stefania getting offered a job than we were 2 years previously when she had applied for the job in the first place.

I can still remember that period of 'limbo' in-between stages 8 and 9 with far from fond memories. One memory I have is that we had friends round for dinner one Sunday and I embarked on a quite aggressive (and as Stefania reminds me each time I recall it, alcohol-fuelled) rant about the incompetent and incomprehensible system of the "*concorso*" that exists in Italy when trying to find work, for the benefit of our Scottish friends who had never had the misfortune of experiencing this blight of Italian culture.

The very next day Stefania got the call. That was it: we really were starting to pack our bags now. Maybe they had heard my rant.

CHAPTER FIVE

La burocrazia

My frustrations with the slow pace of the Italians to do what might seem perfectly simple administrative actions were to continue after we arrived. I am well aware that there have been many newspaper articles, books, jokes, probably television and radio documentaries based on the absurdity of Italian bureaucracy, so all I can do here is share with you my own experiences and leave you to decide for yourself.

Clearly a priority for us when we arrived on Sardinian soil was to find our own place to live. Thankfully, we had an offer from Stefania's parents to stay with them while we found our own place. They lived in Cagliari, the Sardinian capital, where

Stefania had found work, and where we would be setting up our new home. Our naivety had led us to believe that we would find a suitable place to rent fairly quickly and that our imposition on Stefania's parents would be a short-term one.

How wrong we were.

In actual fact, we found a lovely apartment to rent reasonably quickly. That was not the problem. Indeed, we started paying rent almost immediately after we agreed terms and conditions with the landlord, Signor Rossi. The Signori Rossi (that is, Signor Rossi and Signora Rossi), including their 16-year-old daughter Martina, were the nicest landlords one could ever hope to have.

The Rossis would often offer us several foodstuffs, always from their own garden, which had lemon trees, olive trees, fig trees, and pomegranate trees. Practically an orchard. They had their own Sardinian oven (a special kind of oven which is normally built up with bricks and placed outside or on a balcony) which they would use to bake some fresh bread and then pop upstairs with a loaf for us. They were so nice. I even thought that they might just say to us, "Oh, don't worry about the rent this month. We can forget about it this time", but maybe that was wishful thinking on my part. They never did quite say that. Their garden was huge, and the kids had taken the habit, after we had been living there a few months, to go downstairs and ask if they could play in it. The Rossis never complained: indeed, they would host the children with alacrity and on some days the kids would be downstairs for whole afternoons.

The Rossis had built the house we were renting on top of their own property: a two-bedroomed apartment with a huge, sprawling terrace that allowed us to sit and play, hang our washing out, and my favourite activity: eating and drinking outside. All with a fabulous view of the Poetto beach on one side and a view of the nearby mountains on the other.

It is quite common over here to build on top of your own house, usually so that your own children can live there. Indeed, Signor Rossi admitted that was the very reason why he had built the apartment himself. I can't imagine for a nanosecond the same thing happening in the UK. The thought of living above your parents for the rest of your (or your parents') lives just doesn't even come into consideration. In fact, this highlights another cultural difference between here and back home. Most children in the UK can't wait to move out: often as early as when they go to University, or when they find a job (i.e. around 18-19 years old). Here it is very different. It is not uncommon to be living with your parents well into your 30s, even 40s, and only eventually moving out when you get married. Stefania's cousin Maurizio was still living with his mum when he turned 40. He was a lawyer, had a good income and would drive around in his top-of-the-range sports car. He had a lovely girlfriend as well but for some reason he never moved out. His girlfriend eventually got tired of waiting (they had been '*fidanzati*' for about 20 years) and she settled down with someone else. No wonder.

Anyway, to get back to my story: finding the apartment was not the problem. The problem was trying to have us registered with the necessary utilities, in order for us to actually stay there. Unless we wanted to stay in a place without water and electricity.

First, we had to register with an energy company in order for them to provide us with electricity. This is not a straightforward process. In addition to the paperwork for the house that was drawn up with Signor Rossi, we had to provide proof of residency in Cagliari. This is where the trouble begins. Residency status in Italy can be quite a complicated affair. I had yet to formally apply for residency in Italy; however, Stefania knew she would have to do so as soon as possible. For a whole myriad of reasons, her residency in Italy would be essential. The problem is that for anything involving an administrative process in Italy, nothing is simple.

Firstly, Stefania had to inform the Italian Consulate in Edinburgh that she was now living in Cagliari and that her stay (10 years long!) in Scotland had come to an end. Only then could she apply for residency in Italy. A problem, however, was that her residency in Italy, prior to moving to the UK, was not in Cagliari, but in a small town, 60 miles north of Cagliari, called San Vito. Thus, in order to change her residency to that of Cagliari, she had to present herself to the '*Comune*' (the Town Hall) in San Vito, request that her residency be transferred to Cagliari (on production of the tenancy contract), and then go to the *Comune* in Cagliari, where they would issue her with the necessary document. All within the usual working hours (and even then, these places shut down for 4 hours in the afternoon... for a wee rest). Each time one would have to wait in a not insubstantial queue, although how these queues operate is another book in itself – I'm still trying to work out the procedure involved.

At this point, we were able to complete the application for the electricity to be connected to the house. I stress "complete the application", however. This does not mean that the electricity can be connected immediately. The application has to be "processed", which can take several days, in our case, nearly a week. Finally, a letter arrived at the house (where we were not able to live yet), stating that the application had been successful.

If that was considered laborious, then there was more to come. Having us connected for a water supply was just as difficult. However, six weeks after we had signed the tenancy agreement we were in: our new home, a brand-new 2-bedroomed apartment, with a large, lovely terrace and beautiful views of the mountains. We were happy. However, our frustration with setting ourselves up in Cagliari was not finished. I won't begin to tell you the story of how long it took us to buy a car. That was almost as bad. I think in the end it was almost 2 months from us signing the papers until the car was delivered to us.

It's useless me saying to Stefania, "Why is everything here so complicated?", because she just replies, "Why is everything in the UK so simple?". I always assume that 'simple' is better. Maybe I should stop doing that.

CHAPTER SIX

Religione

It would be very difficult to live in Italy and not be touched in some shape or form by religion. From our terrace I can hear the church bells every morning and every evening, calling the parishioners for mass. I don't know why, but it is a comforting sound. It's not that I follow the call for mass and go but knowing that there are others out there who do, seems to provide me with some kind of reassurance strangely.

While I do go to mass occasionally, I don't go as often as I should, but what has been fascinating for me since living over here is that one can see quite clearly how central the church is to life in the community – especially so in the small villages and towns around Cagliari, but also in Cagliari itself. Probably as it used to be in the UK around 40 or 50 years ago (or maybe still is in some remote places that I don't know about).

Each church usually has a football pitch, or a basketball pitch, that is open to all the local youngsters each evening: you will find these pitches packed full in the evenings with young people, many of whom have probably not entered a church in years, but they still have a connection with the parish. The priest is usually around and can often be seen joining in on the games: trying to recruit some extra parishioners while nutmegging them as he passes by.

While statistics would seem to suggest that there are fewer numbers attending church over here than before, it would be difficult to know this, given the packed churches that I have seen since we moved. Maybe there are fewer churches, I don't know, but one certainly does not get the impression that one does in many churches in the UK, where there are about a dozen people sparsely trying to fill a large, empty chapel. Instead the churches I have been to over here are packed full, sometimes with standing room only, often including a young choir with musical accompaniment on guitar, flute and keyboards, and sometimes even drums. The singing is beautiful, sometimes including rather complicated harmonies. The congregation can join in or just sit and listen as they wish. There is a *'bella atmosfera'* and one that makes you want to be part of it, perhaps even if you have been previously ambivalent about organised religion. I would certainly challenge anyone - believers, agnostics, atheists - out there to come along to one of these masses and not feel at least some kind of tingle down their spine.

Our first encounter with the local church and clergy, however, was not an auspicious one. It was a month after we had moved into our new apartment and we had not yet attended mass at the local church, a couple of hundred yards down the road. My parents were over from Scotland for a visit and it was Good Friday. By evening time, in the face of Catholic tradition of abstinence and fasting on Good Friday, we had decided to get pizzas from the local take-away pizzeria. We had not realised the penance we would face for such a decision.

My dad and I popped out to get the pizzas in the car, so that they would still be hot by the time we got home. On the way back from the pizzeria, Stefania called me on the mobile phone. Her voice was frantic, creating panic in me instantaneously:

"There's a procession coming down the street. It's huge. The police are out and everything. They're closing off the roads".

How this all happened in the short while since we left the house, I do not know. There had been a queue at the pizzeria, though we hadn't been away longer than half an hour. In that time, the hundred or so people involved in the procession had gathered outside the church and the police had organised themselves to close off the streets where the procession would be taking place ... including our street.

I don't know if you have ever witnessed one of the Good Friday processions in Italy, or elsewhere for that matter. They are quite serious and sombre affairs, for obvious reasons. To the uninitiated, this day marks the day that Christ was placed on the Cross. A group at the front usually carries a fairly large effigy of the Madonna (almost the size of an adult) and the priest leads the worshippers in a continuous loop of Catholic prayer. The procession can also include the rather odious and distasteful sight of several people dressed in white cloaks and hoods, seemingly in a homage to the Ku Klux Klan, but in fact representing the hundreds of people who did nothing to save Christ from his fate. This one did not include the Ku Klux Klanners, though I did go to one of these said processions in Iglesias, 50 kilometres north west of Cagliari one year, where they are famous for their *"processione di Venerdì Santo"* and I must admit it was quite something and worth a visit, though at the same time very strange.

Anyway, back to my impending situation. Stefania warned me that they had just passed the house and so it would be wise to take a different road home and park the car a little way from the house and walk home, as I would not be able to reach the house by car. Not a problem I thought ... naively. I managed to find a parking spot within a couple of hundred yards from the house.

We got out of the car, my Dad and I, with pizza boxes piled high and a carrier bag full of bottles of beer, and started making our way quickly back to the house. As soon as we turned the corner of the street we were met with the full-on procession coming our way. This was not going to be pretty. The priest was leading the procession, shouting out the prayers, with the worshippers repeating the chants.

What do we do now? We couldn't really turn back – the pizzas were already getting cold and we wouldn't have been able to move the car anyway – so we just had to grin and bear it, and walk stoically through the chanting faithful. We felt so guilty that we couldn't even look them in the eye – heads down, we passed them by, pizza boxes piled high and the beer bottles clanking at the bottom of the plastic bag. At one point I hesitantly looked up and saw about 20 pairs of eyes staring at me in what could only be described as a pontifical air, surely damning me to hell for even thinking of eating pizza and having a beer on Good Friday. I'm sure I even saw some of them shaking their heads...

There is a further twist to this story, however. The following week, my mum and dad were at our home on their own when they heard the doorbell ring, and lo and behold, who was at the door but the priest from the procession the week before. My dad's initial thought was that now he was going to be officially ex-communicated from the church on grounds of pizza eating and beer drinking on Good Friday. However, instead the priest was merely doing his rounds to bless the houses in the parish, as is tradition here after Easter. The priest enters the house, sprays some of his incense around the rooms, including the bedrooms and says a short prayer for the household members. Did the priest recognise my dad from the previous week's events? We can only guess. He never said anything, and my dad certainly kept quiet.

As for the 'spraying' of incense, for those amongst you unaware of this Catholic tradition, this involves swinging an ornamental bronze vase-like container, which emits a fragrant smoke, symbolising the faithful's prayers rising to heaven ... luckily there is not the same tradition of using smoke alarms in houses in Italy, as there is in the UK, otherwise there would be a simultaneous break out of several hundred smoke alarms in the area in the period after Easter – surely triggering a wide scale misinterpretation that Armageddon has begun.

Why are there no smoke alarms in houses in Italy? Stefania explained to me that the houses and walls are made of bricks and stone (and without wallpaper) and since there are no carpets either (all houses have stone or marble tiles as flooring), there is therefore no need for them. But when I probed further to ask if that meant there were never any house fires in Italy, she just ignored me, which usually signifies that she can't explain any further. So, the truth is I don't know why there are no smoke alarms in houses in Italy. I'll need to look into that one.

CHAPTER SEVEN

Cappuccino

About 4 months after we moved, Stefania looked at me one morning and asked, "do you know you're getting fat?" Only it wasn't really a question. Not the nicest comment to begin the day with, but as I looked in the mirror I thought "Mmm, maybe she has a point". Let me put this into perspective. I've been as thin as a rake all my life. As the Scottish expression goes, frequently recited to me by many during my childhood, and even during my adulthood, "I've seen more meat on a butcher's pencil". However, since the move over here, I did begin to put on a bit of weight. In fact, as I weighed myself that morning after Stefania's comment, I discovered that I was the heaviest I had ever been in my life.

Why, you may ask? Well, as far as I can see the answer lies in a particular habit that I took up pretty much immediately after our move, and it's a habit I cannot resist around 10.30-11am each day. I find it almost impossible to get through the morning without a visit to my local bar for a *cappuccino* and a *pasta* (a sweet pastry, that is, not a bowl of spaghetti).

Going to the bar is one of the cultural habits over here that I absolutely adore. The bars themselves are just so ornamental and grandiose that I just feel they're inviting me to go in. It's the open glass cabinets with their marble tops, full of enticing, mouth-watering pastries, of all shapes and sizes, and the huge, monumental, shiny coffee machines lurking in the background behind the bar that just prove too tempting for me.

The pastries are usually filled with either *crema* (not cream but more like custard), *marmellata* (jam) or *cioccolato* (need I translate?), or indeed if you prefer, *vuota* (empty). The different shapes of pastries all have different names, and this is something I was determined to learn quickly so as not to continue to appear like a pre-civilised Neanderthal man at the bar by pointing and grunting to indicate the one I wanted. For example, you may decide to have *una bomba* (a bomb), *una conchiglia* (a shell – my personal favourite), *una pesca* (a peach), *un ventaglio* (a fan) or even *un cannoncino* (a little canon). I just love the idea of walking into your local Greggs in Glasgow and asking politely to the shop assistant, "Can I have a bomb, please?" I can imagine the response. The anti-terrorist squad would be on you before you can say "It's ok, I'll have an empire biscuit instead".

Anyway, this habit is playing havoc with my weight. Most Italians will have a cappuccino and a pasta as their *colazione* (breakfast), which will last them the whole morning until lunchtime. My problem is that I have my breakfast when I get up with the kids (usually a bowl of cereal and a glass of juice) and then top it up with another breakfast mid-morning. Don't be under any illusion here: one of the pastries from the bar and a cappuccino made from whole milk is the equivalent of eating a full pizza. Or so my wife keeps telling me. She is prone to exaggeration at times, but I'm sure she's probably right. But I just can't resist.

One of the most important things in life over here is to identify your preferred bar. This does, and should, take time. There are literally hundreds in close proximity to each other, so you have to carefully consider the merits of each. There are several aspects to this decision-making process that I will try my best to summarise in a series of questions that one has to ask: is there generally a good choice of pastries? Are there still some left if you happen to enter the bar late morning? What's the quality of the pastry like? What's the quality of the cappuccino like? Is the coffee good? Is the milk at the right temperature? Are there tables? Is it always too busy (can't get served or can't find a seat)? Is it always too empty (no atmosphere at all)? Are the employees, including the barista (who makes your cappuccino) pleasant? Do you have to pay for things upfront (not traditionally the case but becoming more common) or can you pay as you leave (preferred)?

You get the picture. It's not a simple process. When Stefania told me once, "no we're not going to that bar because the coffee is rubbish", I didn't really understand what she meant, or how she could make that judgement. Coffee is coffee after all. However, now I know, and I can tell the difference if the coffee isn't quite up to scratch in the bar. In the same way as a British person can tell you straight away if the tea they're drinking is not of a high quality, Italians will do the same with coffee. They're very fussy about their coffee, but then again, I'm very fussy about my tea (most of the tea they sell over here is disgusting – I end up stocking up on proper tea when I'm back in Scotland on holiday). And if truth be told, if I don't provide clear instructions to someone who is making me a cup of tea (i.e. keep the tea bag in for at least 5 minutes, put just a dash a milk in and one sugar), then I end up not drinking it as it tastes awful. Italians do the same with their coffee, which is why when we have friends round to the house I now refuse to make coffee as the ungrateful sods just refuse to drink it, and Stefania has to go away and make it again (what a waste of coffee, it really is).

It's taken me several months, but I have now identified my favourite bar: Bar Casti in Monserrato, a suburb of Cagliari, close to where we live. Bar Casti answers all of those questions positively. The pastries are unbelievably tasty, mainly because Bar Casti has its own *pasticceria* (bakery). They just have a constant stream of fresh pastries come in from the bakery next door so they're usually warm. Delicious. The coffee is good too. It's always busy but never too busy. There are tables and chairs inside and also outside. The staff are pleasant, and they get to know exactly what you want, so you don't even have to ask. The sure sign that you've become a valued patron of the bar is when you don't have to order up your cappuccino: it's always waiting for you at the bar, after you've been to collect your pastry.

This is another important aspect that you have to learn about the bar culture over here: how you order and the order in which you order (if you get my drift). First of all, you must go to the part of the bar where the pastries are and begin to eat your pastry, and only then do you approach the other part of the bar where the coffees and cappuccinos are. A cappuccino should be ordered as a "*cappuccio*", if you want to fit in. Another advantage of being a valued patron of the bar is that you pay as you leave, not as you enter, although this has resulted in a couple of embarrassing episodes for me where I've discovered only after munching my way through several pastries and a couple of cappuccinos that I've come out without my wallet. Still, if you're a patron, it's not a problem, "*Domani, domani signore, non c'è problema*". You can pay the next time you're in.

In the centre of Cagliari there are some bars that are considered historical institutions in the city. One of these bars – and another one of my favourites – is Bar Pirani. I love watching the *baristi* as they serve several hundred *caffé* and cappuccino in the space of 15 minutes (or so it seems). The *paste* are delicious too. You also might bump into some celebrities while you're there. It's not uncommon to see Gigi Riva, the world-famous Italian footballer who played in the 1970 World Cup team that reached the final (and he was instrumental in Cagliari winning the Italian championship that same year).

If you happen to find yourself at Bar Pirani and wish to visit another Cagliari 'institution', then walk straight up the hill from Bar Pirani and you will eventually find yourself on via San Giovanni. In front of you should be one of the oldest *pasticceria* in Cagliari: *Pasticceria Manuel*. It's not a bar. It's simply a *pasticceria* that supplies pastries to many of the city centre bars in Cagliari. However, they have a little shop attached where you can buy your own *bomba alla crema* straight from the oven. In fact, it's a bit of a tradition amongst the Cagliari people to pass by *Pasticceria Manuel* on their way home in the 'wee small hours', as it is open at that time of night. The bakers are working away in order to supply the bars first thing in the morning. However, they don't seem to mind taking a little break to sell you one of their 'famous' pastries as you stumble your way home after a night out. It certainly makes a pleasant change from a Donner Kebab and Chips 'n' Cheese.

Close to *Pasticceria Manuel* and right opposite Bar Pirani is the San Benedetto Market, which is one of the biggest indoor markets in Europe and sells everything from fruit and veg, fresh meat, cheese and a whole lot of other things in between. And a whole floor is dedicated to fresh fish and seafood. It is a wonderful experience just to walk around the San Benedetto Market and take in the atmosphere. You don't have to buy anything, though you might get dragged in by the enticing shouts and chants by the vendors. I love going on a Saturday morning, the busiest day of the week. It is utter chaos, but in a good way. In an Italian way, if I may say so. All you hear is the constant farewell shout of "Buona Domenica" – have a good Sunday! – both from the vendors and their faithful customers alike.

It's important to point out here that one of the basic tenet of bar etiquette, and one that I've seen written about in several other books and web-sites (only because it's true): never order a cappuccino after 11am, in fact, even between 10.30 and 11am would be considered a little strange. If you want to try and blend in with the local culture and not announce yourself as a *straniero*, then never, and I mean never, order a cappuccino after 11am. Italians love to laugh at the *inglesi* who order up a cappuccino in a restaurant after they've just eaten a heavy meal. Ordering a cappuccino in a bar after 11am is frowned upon for a similar reason: it's too close to lunchtime and you shouldn't be having something as heavy as a cappuccino. Instead, you should order a *caffè* or if you want to take a risk, a *caffè macchiato*, i.e. an espresso with a tiny amount of steamed milk, a mini cappuccino if you like.

I did risk ordering a *caffè macchiato* after a meal when I was out for a pizza with my footballing friends, and I've never lived it down. After the meal, the waitress asked confirmation for all those who wanted coffee, which was done by a show of hands, and then I piped up "excuse me, could I possibly have mine *macchiato*?". My goodness, you would've thought by their reaction that I'd just stood up and my trousers had fallen down, revealing Mickey Mouse underpants. They still talk about it. Now I do get the piss taken out of me by my good friends in Scotland for many things, but I can't imagine them saying "Remember that time Fraser ordered a coffee and he wanted a wee bit of milk in it. Oh, what a fool". But there you go. We're in Italy. These things are important.

CHAPTER EIGHT

Calcio

Close to Bar Casti is my local hairdresser (no obvious jokes please: it does require a wee tidy every now and then). Although calling it a hairdresser is like calling Pizza Hut a pizzeria. I think a more accurate description would be barber shop. This was introduced to me by my father-in-law who has been going there for as long as he could remember. The first time I went I thought he was playing a practical joke on me.

We went to a *palazzo* (an apartment building) but instead of going up the stairs to one of the flats, we went down the stairs to the basement, through a dark corridor, and eventually we entered a makeshift barber shop. It was like going back in time. I thought I'd entered a Tardis somewhere along the journey. The mirrors were all old and rusty around the edges. There was a Pirelli calendar on the wall with women in various states of undress (honestly, do they still make these?). The equipment looked like the first prototypes that were designed after electricity was invented. In the background, opera music was blaring out of the stereo. I was bedazzled.

The two barbers were respectively 70 and 68 years old, two brothers, Signor Salvatore and Signor Mario, who had been running their legitimate business for as long as, indeed for longer than, I had been alive. Their clientele were mostly friends and family and their *conoscenti*, who would come along to get their capillary needs attended to, and all at a very reasonable price. Signor Salvatore and Signor Mario were both characters, but in very different ways.

Signor Salvatore, though the eldest, was the more active and energetic of the two (he would do a 10km jog each day, "just to keep myself on top of things"), however he had a fading memory. He would ask me every time I came in to remind him what my name was, as he'd forgotten in between each visit, and eventually I said to him to help him remember that it was very similar to the word "freezer" (a word that is used in Italian as well). So, from then on, I was known as "Freezer". In addition, each time I went he would recount his (seemingly) favourite joke that even though he is getting older now, it hasn't changed the fact that he is still very attracted to women. It's just that he can't quite remember why.

Signor Mario was different: he was not as active physically, but his mind, despite his best efforts not to let on, was very much still in good working order. He was quiet and would always let Signor Salvatore do the talking, but every so often he would come out with a cutting, quick-witted remark that would put anyone and everyone in their place. But he would always do it with a glint in his eye, as if to say, "don't worry, I don't really mean it".

They would talk Sardinian to their aging customers, unless for my benefit when they would switch to Italian, just so I could join in with the joke or story. They always would point out to the other customers that I was Scottish, and how amazing this was, like I was some kind of exotic creature that they'd caught out in the wild during one of their explorations. I just had to sit there and be stared at and prodded like I was a sort of exhibit (I'm joking ... they didn't stare). One of the main topics of conversation when I'm at the barbers is *il calcio* (the football), and in the main, the vicissitudes of the local team, Cagliari.

It is difficult to live over here and not get touched by the football obsession the locals have. Cagliari have a team that play in Serie A, the top division in Italian football. Therefore, since moving here I've had the opportunity to go and see some of the most famous teams in world football: AC Milan, Internazionale (known in the UK, wrongly, as Inter Milan), and Juventus, and that's not to mention plenty of other teams that will be well known to other football enthusiasts: Roma, Lazio, Fiorentina, Sampdoria, Napoli. The list goes on. You can probably sense my child-like excitement just as I type these names.

Luckily, I do like football, therefore, it is not the case that I have had *calcio* forced upon me since we moved here. Quite the contrary, I have embraced it. My brother in-law Flavio is a big Cagliari fan and we go to some of the home games when we can. The atmosphere inside the stadium is unique, or certainly different from my experience of going to the local stadium in Kilmarnock to watch my beloved Killie.

Behind one of the goals stand the very fanatical *tifosi*, known as the *Ultra*. There are two very different views of the *Ultra*: one view would say they are basically football hooligans that cause havoc and destruction wherever they go, and they should be banned from all stadiums. Another view is that they give loyal and unswerving support to their local team, follow them home and away, and provide an electric atmosphere that is unique to Italian football, and at the same time they provide their local team with an extra boost on the field of play. Probably both views have some merit, however, I know one thing: without them, the stadiums would not be the same. Their chanting in unison reaches quite a crescendo, and is quite impressive, although it must be said that some of their banners and songs do leave a lot to be desired in terms of their offensive qualities.

Football is everywhere over here – not just regarding the local team, Cagliari, but also there is great support for *gli azzurri* – the Italy national team. As I said in the first chapter they are known as *gli azzurri* because of the azure blue colour of their shirts, which in fact was chosen for the national football team as it was representative of the Italian Royal family, before Italy became a republic in 1946. Despite becoming a republic, the football team decided to keep with the shirts. The year after we moved to Sardinia the excitement was building up towards the 2010 World Cup, and as the holders of the biggest and most famous sporting competition in the world, much was expected from *gli azzurri*.

I often get asked by people about what I see as the differences between living in Italy and living in the UK. One of the differences that I often highlight, some might argue a little over-simplistically, is that the Italian culture revolves around food while the British culture revolves around drink. A perfect illustration of that is the promotion leaflet that was being put round by a large supermarket over here in celebration of the World Cup arriving. Now I'd happily be corrected, but in my experience in the UK these leaflets announcing the arrival of the World Cup usually do so by offering cut-price cans of lager and other alcoholic drinks. Instead, the local supermarket was using the World Cup to announce that they were offering half price pizza and pasta. I kid you not. This is absolutely true. The pizza and pasta came in the three colours of the Italian flag (green, white and red) in celebration of the *azzurri's* attempt to regain the World Cup.

Unfortunately, the 2010 World Cup all ended in tears for Italy – quite literally in our household. This was Luca's first real World Cup in which he followed all the matches closely, and sadly, Italy were deeply disappointing and probably played their worst World Cup in over 40 years, going out in the first group stage[1]. I tried to console him by saying that I had to endure the same experience as a 6-year-old when Scotland were cruelly knocked out of the World Cup in 1978 after beating Holland 3-2 in that memorable game when Archie Gemmell dribbled round almost the whole Dutch team and chipped the goalkeeper. The emotional scars remain, especially because, for us Scots, even qualification for a major football tournament remains a distant dream. The last one we qualified for was in 1998 in France. At least he has many more World Cups and European Championships to

---

[1] I should add here that this disastrous World Cup was arguably superseded by Italy's performance at the 2014 World Cup where they were again eliminated at the group stage, and even more so by their failure to even qualify for the 2018 World Cup.

look forward to and hope that Italy can erase those scars by winning other tournaments in the future. Given my semi-Italian nationality, an Italian win might even erase my own Scottish-induced scars.

Luca is very proud of his Scottish identity and in fact it is one of the first things he'll announce to some new friends that's he's just met, for example if he's down the park for a game of football. He'll look each of them in the eye and say "*sono scozzese*" (I'm Scottish), almost like a threat, as if it might make him immune from some overly enthusiastic tackles. It certainly comes across as "don't mess with me". However, one question he doesn't like, and he seems to get asked it often, is: if Scotland were playing Italy, who would you support? He usually replies, "a draw", however, when pressed and on one occasion he's even been asked: what if it were a knockout game, for example, for qualification for the World Cup and only one team could go through? The wee man pulled through and replied "Scotland". I think he even punched his heart as he said it. Or maybe that was my imagination. Either way, he's clearly understood the pain that I've been carrying since 1998.

CHAPTER NINE

Trasporti

I hate stereotypes because they tend to over-generalise people at the expense of those who do not follow the stereotype, and, in addition, they often signify a narrow-mindedness in the person who holds the stereotype – something that I despise ... however ... I now wish to include an exception in that statement ... I think the stereotype about Italian drivers is true. Even after living in Italy for years I still get shocked, bewildered and bemused by the driving feats witnessed on a daily basis over here.

Firstly, there's the zebra crossing. This is an experience in itself. The first time I had to cross the road at a zebra crossing I was convinced the guy must have been a drunk driver. By the 8th time, I realised that this is just what they do over here. Let me explain. I think in the UK we make far too many naïve assumptions about walking across a road at a zebra crossing. First of all, we assume that when a pedestrian is standing waiting at a zebra crossing that the cars will stop to let the person cross. Secondly, we assume that when the pedestrian places his or her feet onto the road, and begins to cross, that the cars will wait until the person has reached the other side of the road (or at the very least passed the driver's side of the road) before taking off again. How could we be so stupid?

In Italy, if you decide to cross the road at a zebra crossing, you are basically playing a road safety version of Russian Roulette. The cars here do not stop to let pedestrians cross the road – they try to swerve around you, as if you were some kind of mobile traffic cone, getting in the way of their route. I have not yet discovered what the point of the black and white lines is – they might as well have saved their paint.

As a pedestrian, or perhaps I should specify, as a foreign, non-Italian pedestrian (since crossing the road at a Zebra crossing does not seem to fluster the locals so much), the whole thing is a terribly frightening experience. You tentatively place one of your feet on the road in the vain hope that the approaching cars will stop, and instead, when you realise that this is not going to happen, you take one step after another, frantically looking in both directions for advancing vehicles of various shapes and sizes who look as if they're trying to take you out, much like a bowling ball taking out a set of 'pins'. It's crazy.

Don't assume that it is only as a pedestrian that you might encounter some danger on the roads over here. Driving itself is also fraught with danger, mostly from other drivers. While it's possibly true that our own Highway Code is no longer respected in the same way as it was in the past, there are at the very least some general rules that are followed by drivers in the UK. One might say that, in general, there does exist at least some degree of mutual respect between drivers in the UK.

I remember this was wonderfully parodied by a stand-up comedian some years ago – I forget who exactly – when he described the British driver squeezing through the tiniest of gaps in the road only to lift his hands off the steering wheel and risk a collision in order to salute the driver in the other car who ceded their position to allow for the manoeuvre. Here in Italy, instead, there is only one overarching rule for the road … do whatever you want … as long as you don't cause a crash. Not so much the Highway Code but the Whateverway Code.

How they use roundabouts here is just mind-boggling. The whole idea of what to do at a roundabout just seems to be beyond the average driver's comprehension. The drivers approaching the roundabout don't seem to understand that you must give way to the traffic already on the roundabout (in Italy, this is the traffic coming from the driver's left). Instead, they just enter the roundabout without looking to see if there is traffic coming from the left, and they usually do this just as you're trying to move lane to come off the roundabout. A bit of "come and go" is required so as to avoid an accident (usually meaning I have to slow down and let the other driver pass).

I break out into a cold sweat every time I'm approaching a roundabout over here. I imagine that it's the same level of fear and trepidation that a bungee jumper feels just as they're being tied to the rope. "Everything should be fine, shouldn't it? But what if something goes wrong? What's going to happen this time?". One day I got caught in a near gridlock because a car was trying to come off a large roundabout at an exit, but another car was going past that particular exit in the inside lane. Neither driver budged, and they just stopped their respective cars to argue the point about who was in the right, rather than just trying to sort it out by yielding their position. While this went on for several minutes, the cars started to back up, and the roundabout was soon full of vehicles all the way around. I think we sat there for around 20 minutes while the problem was sorted out.

The use of the horn (*il clacson*) is a language in itself. After studying it for several years I can now distinguish between five distinct levels of horn use:

1) *a quick toot*: Just to let you know I'm here so that you don't reverse out of that parking space or pull out in front of me at that junction

2) *a slightly longer toot*: I'm behind you at the traffic lights and the lights turned to green 0.2 seconds ago and you're still stationary

3) *a longish hoot and repeated several times*: what the hell is going on here? would someone get a move on? We've been stationary for 4.5 seconds and no-one is moving

4) *a still longer hoot and repeated several times*: for fuck sake, this is ridiculous. There is a serious problem here in the traffic. Maybe if we all hoot together for several minutes then this will surely resolve the problem. (Note that this particular tooting behaviour is also reserved for the common experience of having to alert someone who has double-parked in front of you that it is high time that they returned to their vehicle and let you out. Rarely will an apology from the 'double-parker' be offered. It's normal and expected that you double-park, so what's your problem? Why the need to apologise?)

5) *hooting all the way as you drive, repeated several times over, and in unison with others*: this is reserved for special events, most commonly for a wedding and is done in convoy.

It took me a while to learn these distinctions. If you get it wrong, you could be in serious trouble.

Another thing I feel compelled to talk about is the proliferation of two tiny modes of transport over here: one that will be familiar to most readers, and one that may not be so familiar. I'll start with the much loved "scooter" or "moped". Most readers will be familiar with the *Vespa*, which was somewhat glamorised in the 1960s as the only cool way to go around on two wheels (also made fashionable by Nanni Morretti: those of you who are Italian film buffs will know exactly who I mean). *Vespa* translates as Wasp, the name ingeniously chosen as the scooter *buzzes* about town.

Scooters are so common over here that when I'm out and about I sometimes wonder if I've taken too many of my plurification pills in the morning. They are everywhere, and most of the time (I think I may be a little biased here) driven by very attractive young girls. I don't think I'll ever see in my lifetime in the UK as many young females driving what is almost the equivalent of a motorbike. It is part of the culture over here, and not necessarily a good part of the culture, mostly because of the unfortunate frequency there is of serious, often fatal, accidents involving the scooter.

It has to be said that they do drive the scooters in an incredibly reckless and hazardous manner (though as you will have understood by now, this is not exclusive to the average scooter driver). They will nip in and out of the smallest of gaps that appear in the traffic, usually at high speed, and often without any due care for the heart condition of the other drivers (no, I am not referring again to the abundance of beautiful girls who drive them). At least they are now wearing helmets after a hugely successful public awareness campaign by the Italian government in the last 10 years. The only disadvantage of this is that I don't manage to catch a glimpse of a full and complete appearance of those driving ...

The scooter drivers that do the most reckless manoeuvres are the pizza delivery guys: they are the experts when it comes to getting around as quickly as you can, squeezing in and out of gaps, overtaking when they shouldn't and even going on the pavements in order to get to their destination quicker. However, they are delivering the national culinary treasure, so perhaps they should be forgiven. Those of you who have eaten cold pizza know exactly what I mean.

The other mode of transport that I feel I cannot avoid mentioning is the tiny *Ape*. The *Ape*, which translates literally as "bee" (it is made by the same manufacturer as the *Vespa*: ingenious again), is basically a 3-wheeled scooter (one at the front, two at the back), with a kind of mini-pick-up truck attached in such a way that you don't actually notice that it's a scooter underneath. It's a very strange looking vehicle, in fact, so strange, that I am sure my description is probably one of the worst you will ever read, to the extent that I am confident you will still have no clue what I'm talking about here. If you have ever been to Italy, however, and driven a few miles out of the city into the countryside, then you will know exactly what I'm referring to. Once you drive approximately 15 miles out of the city, you find them everywhere. The reason being is that they are incredibly handy for the many Italians who still have a very close relationship to the *"terra"* (i.e. the land), such that they need them to transport whatever fruit or vegetables they might be growing in their nearby *"orto"* (allotment). Of course, they are also used to transport other things too, like furniture for example (as long as it's no larger than a two-seater sofa).

Anyway, whether it be a *Vespa*, an *Ape*, a van, a bus or just an ordinary car, the point is that these vehicles can come from nowhere and suddenly swerve out in front of you, maybe overtaking from the inside or crossing over from the lane going in the opposite direction (because the driver felt it was going to be easier and quicker to do a U turn in a busy street rather than trying to change direction in a safer, more sensible manner).

Since living over here I am constantly on the look-out for Dastardly and Muttley, and Penelope Pitstop, as I'm sure I've inadvertently found myself being caught up in an episode of Wacky Races. No, I'm not joking.

CHAPTER TEN

Il clima

It's November and it's still hot over here. The other day the local pharmacy had the temperature registered as 28oC, around 82oF. Not absolutely burning hot, but for a wee boy from Kilmarnock it's certainly something I'm not used to in the month of November. You could easily go to the beach, though very few locals do at this time of the year, as 28oC is actually considered too cold, would you believe. If it were around 28oC in Scotland everyone would be walking around in short sleeves and shorts, and a few hardy types might even go "taps aff", that is, going around bare-chested, often sporting their tattoos. And as for the men... (sorry, totally predictable, but I couldn't resist).

The fact is, the climate (*il clima*) here is fantastic, and there's no getting around it. I don't say this to rub it in your face or to make you jealous (if you live in the UK), but it's just a fact. We're almost 2000 miles closer to the equator compared to most of you reading this, so it's obvious that we're going to have better weather. My dear old dad used to try and compete, but he was wasting his time. Conversations over the phone would go more or less like this:

My Dad: *"Oh it's a gorgeous day here son. Absolutely glorious. It'll be much the same weather as you're having"*.

Me: *"Oh really. What's the temperature like?"*

My Dad: *"Oh I've no idea son, but it's glorious. The sun's splitting the sky"*.

Me: *"Well, here it was 30oC yesterday and it looks like it'll be much the same today"*.

My Dad: *"Oh I'm sure it's about the same over here son"*.

Me: *"Dad, it's October. Scotland has never had temperatures of 30oC in October, I can assure you"*.

My Dad: *"Well, it'll no' be far off it son"*.

I checked the day after. It was 15oC in Scotland that day.

You see, the thing is, there are lots of positive and negatives about living in the south of Italy. I've only touched on a few negatives so far, but I can assure you there are many more to come. However, the one big positive is the climate. When Stefania used to get down and depressed with the Scottish climate I didn't really appreciate how bad it was for her. After all, I had lived in Scotland most of my life and I didn't know any different. My view was "*just get on with it*", since that's what I had to do all my life. After having lived in Sardinia for a few years I began to fully appreciate how difficult it must have been for her.

The climate has such a huge impact on so many different aspects of your life here. It's not simply a matter of "*oh, it's a lovely day today, isn't it?*". It's so much more than this. It affects what you eat, how you eat (i.e. usually outside), how much time you spend outdoors generally, the amount of exercise you do, whether you can go down the beach, and your general mood and temperament. And it affects all of these aspects in a positive direction. If you take that away from someone who has been used to it all their life, of course it's going to have an impact. And not necessarily for the better. Indeed, if we were ever to move back to Scotland I would find the change in climate difficult to cope with myself, despite putting up with the Scottish climate for the first 36 years of my life.

The principal thing about the climate over here is the fact that, for around six months of the year - from May through to October - life mostly revolves around going to the *"mare"* – the beach. I'll be honest, before moving here I would not have described myself as much of a beach lover. Most of my early memories of going to the beach in Scotland are filled with images of horizontal rain, gale force winds and running to the car for cover. I tended to concur with the Billy Connolly view that, when it comes to the sea, we just shouldn't be there. We spent millions of years evolving to try and get out of the sea, so why are we now rushing to get back in? Things in there sting you, bite you, wrap themselves around you – just get in your way. The sand gets everywhere – in your clothes, in the car, back in the house, not to mention in creases of your body that you didn't even know existed – and added to the fact that when one has Scottish blue skin that doesn't react well to the Sardinian sun, you begin to understand what I mean.

However, after a few years of going down the beach almost constantly from May to October, gradually, my opinion has started to change. I can now appreciate the joys of going down the beach. I love the culture there is of coming back from work and going down the beach in the evening – for me the best time to go is between 5.30 and 8pm. The sea here is truly amazing – absolutely beautiful. The colour of the water is a clear, translucent, celestial blue that I thought only existed in digitally enhanced photographs. I have truly never seen water this colour. The beaches of the Costa Rei (the King's Coast) in the south-east of the island – only a 45-minute drive from Cagliari – were recently voted by a Lonely Planet survey as being in the top 10 beaches of the world, beating the likes of the Seychelles, and the beaches of the Caribbean. It's not difficult to see why.

The colour of the sea has an inviting quality to it – you just feel like it'd be rude not to go in – a feeling I never experienced when going down the beaches in Ayrshire as a child in the 1970s. It also cools you down considerably, a welcome experience during those oppressively hot days during the height of the summer. The view of the surrounding coastline while you're in the water is also spectacular, and I shouldn't forget some of the spectacular views you experience while laying on the beach sunbathing.

There is a beach etiquette that you must learn, though. The sand, in my experience anyway, you just learn to put up with, but also you get more adept at avoiding it getting everywhere. Getting from the beach to the car, in normal clothes and sand-free is an art form and I'm learning from the masters. Indeed, getting changed from normal clothes into your swimming costume is an art form too. One day I saw what looked to me like four work colleagues arriving at the beach in their work clothes and within approximately one minute they were all sitting on their towels, in their costumes, taking in the sun. It was like watching Mr Bean doing it only without the laughs and the clumsiness. This was serious. And it was amazing to watch. It was done in a discreet way – no unsightly body parts were exposed during the exercise.

One of the main things about beach etiquette is knowing the dimensions of personal beach space, in other words, where do you set up your umbrella and towels? The locals just know instinctively: where would be too close, where would be too far away, such that you're wasting the beach space. Of course, for the first few months, I didn't have a clue and was always setting up too close or too far away. And it's important to get it right. I now have a rough idea. I asked Stefania if they offer any training courses in beach etiquette, especially for foreigners. She didn't laugh. She just looked at me and said, "You'll learn".

Other aspects to beach etiquette are mostly common sense: never scroll your sand-filled towel too close to the other bathers, and never allow your children to play with any form of ball game too close to them either. Always make sure you have a pair of beach sandals (NEVER try to walk across the beach in your bare feet or you'll probably end up in hospital – either for the heat or for any debris hanging around waiting to injure you). And finally, always make sure you take your litter away with you. Keeping the beaches clean is important to

Sardinians, as it's the attraction of its splendid beaches that makes a significant contribution to the local economy. Recently there was an episode in one of the beaches close to Cagliari where a local confronted a tourist who had opened a tin of tuna, drained the oil into the sea and then buried the tin in the sand. The local embarked on a half-hour lecture pointing out to the disgraced tourist the folly of her actions. The local's reprimand towards the tourist went on for so long that eventually part of the scene was video-recorded by someone on their mobile phone and the video was put on YouTube. It began to trend, and the 'reprimander' became (quite literally) a local hero. I doubt whether the tourist will be back soon. 'Good riddance' say the locals!

A related problem is that many tourists take away with them some of the Sardinian sand as some kind of souvenir. The problem has become so great that the Sardinian government have now introduced legislation that allows airport officials to fine tourists around €1000 if they catch them sneaking out of the island with a sample of sand in their hand luggage.

Another thing you have to learn about 'beach life' over here is how to put up your umbrella in the most inconspicuous way possible. I'm not very good at that, though I am getting better. I still remember an experience that happened to me during the first summer after we moved. We went down the beach, and while Stefania was trying to quickly put the sun cream on the kids, I took it upon myself to get the umbrella positioned and assembled.

You see a thing that does annoy me about here, and I often experience it at the beach, is the fact that people just don't consider it rude to stare at you. While battling away with the umbrella, this guy was staring at me for – I kid you not – about 5 minutes, without a blink. Stefania said there may have been two reasons for this: 1) I had set up too close, though the beach was fairly empty and, I thought anyway, I was a reasonable distance from him, or (as was more likely) 2) he was enjoying my 'performance' of trying to get the umbrella up in a smooth, trouble-free manner. Bastard! Another thing is the linear fashion in which the umbrellas are assembled. It's like a geometrical vision. They're all perfectly equidistant from each other, in rows and columns, almost like a matrix. Then I come along and ruin the pattern entirely. Maybe the guy was right to stare and intimidate me.

One of our favourite beaches is near Muravera, on the east coast, called Torre Salinas. It's near the Costa Rei, but nowhere near as busy, even during the peak periods in July and August. The water is beautiful, the fine, fine sand is golden and soft, and there are also the *scogli*. Finding a beach with *scogli* is important. I can only translate the concept of *scogli* as big, huge rocks that you find next to the beach. I looked up *scogli* in my massive Collins Italian-English dictionary and it says "cliff, cragg, rock" but that doesn't really capture it for me. The *scogli* are so much more than that. They are a source of great entertainment for the kids – either to fish or just to jump from into the water. Even for the little ones: in-between the *scogli* there are little pools for them to paddle in. The beach at Torre Salinas has some great *scogli*. Once you find a beach that you like, with clean water, fine sand, and some great *scogli*, you patronise it in a possessive way. Torre Salinas has the added bonus of a tower that you can quite easily climb up and it gives you the most amazing view of the coastline. A photographer's dream. Torre Salinas, or indeed whichever beach you patronise in this way during the summer months, becomes a home from home. However, in Sardinia we are really lucky. There are literally hundreds of fantastic beaches to choose from, and so we do tend to make our way around some of them during that summer period from May to October.

I know there are some fine beaches in Scotland. I can hear my mum shouting down the phone at me already as soon as she's read this book, "you've been to Luskentyre beach in Harris: you know it's amazing". And of course, there are other beaches around the west coast of Scotland, and in the Hebrides in particular, that are just as beautiful. I'm not denying that. However, first of all, here in Sardinia there are hundreds, if not thousands, of beaches like Luskentyre, and secondly you can go down and use their 'facilities' on more than a handful of days each year. Still, it must be said that in Scotland's favour at least there's not the same pressure on following rigid beach etiquette. You can put up your umbrella wherever the hell you want. And you can take half an hour too. No-one will be staring. But they might be talking about you as you do it, "What is that guy doing? Putting up a beach umbrella in October? Doesn't he know it's only 15oC?".

CHAPTER ELEVEN

Buon lavoro!

Italians have a salutation for everything – not just for the commonly used *"Buongiorno!"* or *"Buona sera!"*, or even *"Buon viaggio!"*, as you're about to embark on a journey. It is important when entering a shop, a pizzeria, the doctor's surgery, or any other public building to shout out *"Buongiorno!"*, even if they're complete strangers. It's expected that you do so. You would be considered rude if you didn't (although it is not considered rude to barge your way in front of others rather than form an orderly queue: sorry, that's another story, for another day).

There are many more of these kinds of phrases, the most interesting ones are usually said when saying goodbye to someone, depending on the conversation you've just been having. Two of my personal favourites are *"Buona permanenza!"*, which is "Have a good stay!" and *"Buon proseguimento!"*, which could probably best be translated as "Whatever happens to you next, I hope it's good!". Hardly an expression you would be shouting to friends or colleagues as you run past them on the way to catch a train.

I've even been in a situation where I met a friend in the parking area of the shopping centre and he said to me *"Buona spesa"* just after we exchanged a few words of conversation. It basically means "Have a good shop!". My God. Thanks for the sentiment. Actually, he clearly knew what I was in for: Stefania and I were looking for new clothes for a wedding, so he understood my impending torture precisely.

Something that has confused me somewhat since living over here is when to use *"Buongiorno"* ("Good morning!") and when to use *"Buona sera"* ("Good evening!"). I don't know why but the Italians - or maybe this is a Sardinian thing - rarely, if ever, use the salutation *"Buon pomeriggio"* ("Good afternoon!"). *"Buongiorno"* lasts through to about lunch time, or even a little after, say 2pm, after which you have to switch to *"Buona sera"*. It just seems absurd to me that I should be saying "Good evening" at 2 o'clock in the afternoon. But when I say *"Buon pomeriggio"* the locals just look at me as if I'm wearing a Batman costume (actually, if I were wearing a Batman costume they would probably look at me with less bewilderment). On a few occasions, I have been a little confused and said "*Buongiorno*" in the afternoon, basically because it comes naturally to me since it's still daylight. Again, I get the looks and the confused stares (although I did have my Batman costume on that day).

Another expression that is used a lot over here is "*Buon lavoro!*". "*Buon lavoro!*" literally (though not grammatically) translates as "Have a good work!". Even if we translate the phrase into more grammatically correct English, for example, "Enjoy your work!" or "Have a good day at your work!", it is never an expression that is used commonly in the UK or in other English-speaking countries (as far as I'm aware). One might consider it ironic that the expression "*Buon lavoro!*" is used so frequently over here in a context where unemployment is rife and job opportunities are few and far between.

However, my father-in-law once offered me a logical explanation. He told me that the use of "*Buon lavoro!*" emerged in the period after the Second World War where many were having problems finding work. It was used as an expression of good will to another, as a more specific substitute for the more commonly used "*Buona fortuna!*" ("Good luck!"). He told me that "*Buon lavoro!*" had two pragmatic meanings that still apply today: (1) "I hope you will find some work today" (for those out of work) and (2) "I hope your work goes well today and that you will not lose your job" (for those who do work). So, it covers all bases! It particularly resonated with me in the first 6 months or so after we moved as I was still looking for work. In fact, people seemed to be saying it to me all the time, including complete strangers as I was walking down the street. I kept asking myself: How do they know about my predicament? It was probably just my paranoia again.

Nevertheless (or maybe *because of* all these lovely sentiments), about 6 months after we moved I finally found a "*lavoro*". I was offered a job at Cagliari University to work on a research project exploring the possible benefits of bilingual children who speak minority languages. Sardinian as a language is not as widely spoken as it used to be, and in fact, some claim that it is a dialect and not a language, even though it has been officially recognised as a language by the European Community Charter for Regional and Minority Languages. There are still pockets of Sardinian-speaking areas, mostly rural, where children are being brought up as bilingual, that is, Sardinian is spoken in the home and Italian is taught in school. The teaching of Sardinian is not as formalised as it is in many other countries where minority languages are spoken. For example, for the research project, I also had to do a comparison with the development of Gaelic in Scotland, where one can receive a formal education in a Gaelic-speaking school. However, the Sardinian language is very much part of the Sardinian cultural identity in these rural, mountainous areas, and I'm fascinated by it. Just as well – I found myself researching the topic for a living over the following 2 years.

On one of my first days of the job, I had to drive 3 hours north of Cagliari to the small, picturesque town of Dorgali, right in the heart of Sardinia, to meet the head-teacher of the local primary school, who had been recommended to me as a potential collaborator in the research. Dorgali was considered one of a few remaining places where Sardinian is still widely spoken. It took me approximately 3 minutes to fall in love with the place.

Dorgali is right in the middle of a mountain range and has spectacular views as soon as you enter from the west. The town is encircled by a road that basically takes you right round the boundary – almost like a modern city ring-road, only much more picturesque. It took me a couple of 'laps' before I realised the circular aspect of the road, almost like a goldfish swimming round its bowl, as I said to myself "I'm sure I've been here before". Once you're in the town, you quickly get a sense that it is a tourist haven, and you begin to understand why. The town is full of little independent shops, many selling local arts and crafts and produce, but it is the setting that clearly attracts the tourists. Regardless of where you are, you look up and are caught by the steep high mountain ranges, seemingly just above your head.

Luckily for me the head-teacher, Angela, was supportive of the research and agreed to have the school's pupils and parents participate. Not only that, but she also invited me back to her home for lunch. When I say lunch, I don't mean a sandwich and a cup of tea. She called her husband – also a teacher – to go home a bit early and start preparing. Schools finish over here at 1.30pm. We sat down to eat around 2pm. Three hours and five courses later, we were still sitting at the dinner table over coffee, *mirto* (a Sardinian sweet liquor made from myrtle berries, usually served straight from the freezer) and *dolci sardi* (little Sardinian cakes). Only then did I start to think about how much I had had to drink and how I was going to get back to my hotel.

A proper dinner over here, especially when guests are round, usually consists of the following: firstly an *"aperitivo"* (this can be an alcoholic drink or a *"bitter"*, which is a fizzy, red non-alcoholic beverage, with a slightly bitter taste), usually accompanied with nibbles, followed by the *"antipasti"* (for example, dried cured meats, roasted vegetables, olives and bread) with an accompanying glass of wine. Next, the *"primo piatto"* (first course - more often than not, this is a plate of pasta, but can also be a rice-based dish like risotto or even soup), with the wine glass refilled. Then, the *"secondo piatto"* (second course - usually meat or fish), with a *"contorno"* (side dish - for example, salad or vegetables), and again more wine. After the *secondo piatto*, there is always fresh fruit, usually grown locally, placed in the centre of the table. Finally, there is coffee, a liqueur (*mirto* or *limoncello* is common over here in Sardinia) and something sweet – either the "*dolci sardi*" or "*mignon*" (tiny little pastries, like the ones you find in the bar only much smaller versions). Sometimes your host might even have prepared something at home, like a *tiramisù* or a *budino* (almost like a crème caramel).

After all of that, I decided that it was best not to take the car back to the hotel. In fact, it was down a steep hill from Angela's house – I thought I might as well roll back to the hotel instead and pick up the car the following morning. As I walked home it reminded me of my father's friend, Ian, who claimed that the only phrase that one needs to learn when visiting other countries is "do these railings lead to my hotel?".

The following morning as I was driving back to Cagliari, I began thinking about the kind of salutation I would receive from my ex-colleagues in Scotland if I were to tell them of my first day on the job. The most polite comment I could think of was "You call that work?". And then I thought of my dear old Gran, what she might say if she were still around, probably along the lines of "Away and get a real job son". I can't think many would be willing to offer the equivalent of a "*Buon lavoro!*". Anyway, I can't complain, I was thinking - things are starting to look positive. "*Buona permanenza*" I said to myself out loud as I was driving.

CHAPTER TWELVE

Zanzare

Just when I thought things were beginning to look up, I hadn't considered the might of the *"zanzara"*, and what it would do to my life over here. *Zanzare* (plural) are little mosquito-type insects that come out at night, and thrive during the summer months. They're not unlike the Scottish midge, only much, much worse. I hate them. I didn't know there was so much hatred in me until I came across the *zanzara*. I really, really hate them. They are the bane of my life. I detest them so much it's difficult to put into words. They are scum. The lowest of the low. They should be castrated. I hope they all die in a tragic road accident.

Do you think I'm exaggerating? Try living here

for, say 2 months, and you'll feel exactly the same as I do. They are blood suckers. Literally. And when one of these wee things, that on first sight you might think are so harmless, enters the house, or your bedroom, your whole life turns upside down. Well, not quite. Maybe I am exaggerating now. But that's how it feels. You can't sleep, you can't relax, you get worried about the number of bites you'll have in the morning. They are a nightmare. Honestly. In fact, I now have nightmares about them in my sleep. They have infected my whole consciousness. Their whole existence revolves around torturing me. Have you understood yet? I hate these wee bastards. I've tried cream, sprays, nets, everything, they still get me.

When one of these little buggers enters the house, all other priorities fall by the wayside and the killing of the *zanzara* takes over. When trying to follow their flight in order to swat them, I'm convinced they have managed to get their hands on a Harry Potter invisible cloak, which they use at random, making it even more difficult for you to see them. Now you see it, now you don't. They are so annoying. Bastards. I really, really hate them.

They have an infuriating buzzing sound: that's all you can hear at night when trying to sleep. As soon as I hear that familiar buzz, that's me. I switch the lights on, swatter at the ready. Stefania starts to stir as I'm climbing on the bed looking valiant, positioning myself in order to kill the wee bugger.

After about 15 minutes, I give up. I switch the lights back off, get back in my bed in the vain hope that it's maybe flown out of the room. I start to drift off to sleep again ... ah lovely ... buzz, buzz, buzz. No way. Again, the same scenario. Lights on, wife angry, me going mad. Again, the same result: Lauchlan 0 - Zanara 1 (home defeat). They hide away because they know I'm going to get them. In the morning, I wake up with bites everywhere: my arm, my leg, even my head gets them. I think I'm starting to understand – maybe it's not all good stuff over here. Maybe, there are some downsides as well.

There are insects, beasties, animals and even reptiles that I encounter over here that I'm just not used to. There are geckos everywhere. Or, as we call them in Scotland: 'a wee lizardy thing'. Upon first seeing one crawling around our terrace not long after we moved I must admit I had a wee moment (read: was a complete jessie - I think I actually shrieked). Now I'm completely used to seeing them. In fact, they become your pals, especially as they are very practical at keeping the insect population down around the house. They even keep the *zanzare* away (though not entirely, I'm afraid to say).

Another thing that exists over here is a *calabrone*. I looked up *calabrone* in my big Collins Italian-English Dictionary and it said "hornet". I'm telling you, it is not a hornet. I've never seen a hornet the size of a fucking DOG. I still remember vividly the first time I encountered a *calabrone* over here. It was summer, and the windows were wide open and all of a sudden, this huge flying insect came speeding into our living room. I don't swear often, and never swear in front of the kids, but the words, "WHAT THE FUCK WAS THAT?" just automatically escaped from my mouth, without me thinking. And it wasn't a request for information. More a cry for help. Unfortunately, Stefania decided to go for the first interpretation.

"It's a *calabrone*", she said calmly.

"A WHAT? LISTEN, I DON'T CARE WHAT THE FUCK IT IS. GET IT OUT OF MY IMMEDIATE ENVIRONMENT ... NOW!".

"Oh for goodness sake, Fraser. It's only a little insect".

"LITTLE? LITTLE? ARE YOU MESSING WITH ME? DO YOU KNOW THE DEFINITION OF LITTLE? LOOK IT UP. IT MEANS SMALL, DIMINUITIVE, MINISCULE, TINY, PETITE. THAT THING IS NONE OF THESE THINGS. IT'S MASSIVE. YOU KNOW: BIG, LARGE, HUGE, GIANT, ENORMOUS. GET IT OUT OF HERE.

Stefania, shaking her head in contempt and, it must be said, a slight air of derision and ridicule, calmly and efficiently swatted the thing out of the room with a newspaper. I'm sure the Rossi family who live downstairs, our landlords, must have thought I was having a complete meltdown. Well, they weren't far wrong.

The other insects that you find in great number over here are "*pesciolini*" (translates literally as little fish, although they are actually insects). I don't know the technical name for them. I asked Stefania and she replied "Oh, those little things. They don't have a technical name". Which means she doesn't know. Anyway, they are funny little insects and completely harmless, but you find them everywhere, but only at night. During the day, there is absolutely no sign of them, but if you happen to get up during the night (for example, to deal with a wet bed or a thirsty child) then you see them slithering along across the floor trying to reach their destination. There is nothing to them: they are genuinely tiny and if you happen to kill one of them, they seem to be made of dust. Weird.

On the more positive side, one thing I do love over here is the night-time sound of the crickets. There's nothing I like more than sitting out in the terrace in Cagliari, late at night, where the distinctive, yet strangely comforting, sound of the crickets' singing fills the nocturnal silence, a constant reminder to me that I now live in a Mediterranean country.

I may be wrong here, but I recall reading about an (incredibly stupid) guy who loved the sound of the crickets so much he purchased and had imported about a 1000 of them for his garden, despite living somewhere in England. After about two weeks the crickets all died out as they couldn't survive in the harsher English climate compared to what they were used to. Obviously. The guy forked out several thousand pounds on a two-week cricket spectacle. What a fanny. Or maybe I'm being harsh. Maybe he knew all along they would only last a couple of weeks. Or maybe he didn't. Let's just stick with being harsh and call him a complete tosser.

As for animals, well Sardinia is quite well known for its wild boar, or "*cinghiali*". I still remember on one occasion when we were out on a country walk near San Vito and we turned a bend and were suddenly met with three wild hogs standing right in front us. About 10 metres right in front of us. I could spot another potential meltdown happening. Stefania knew how to handle it though. We just calmly turned back the way we came as if we had just decided that it was time to do so, as opposed to screaming and running for our lives (which is what I was about to do).

Part of the culture over here is to hunt the *cinghiali*: for food, not for sport. In other words, it is totally different to the role that fox hunting plays in the UK. Also, hunting *cinghiali* is not reserved for the upper classes. Anyone can do it. It's not something I've been tempted by, although I know many who do. Flavio, my brother-in-law, doesn't hunt either but his dad does, and one time he gave us a huge piece of *cinghiali* meat as a present. It was surprisingly good, though you have to cook it carefully so that it is still tender.

Another part of the culture over here is eating horsemeat. It's considered a delicacy. A couple of years ago I remember there was an outcry in the UK as they had detected horsemeat in some supermarket burgers. People over here were saying, "what's your problem? The burgers will be much tastier". My dad, who came over to visit us several times, always refused to eat it. He was a butcher, but he just couldn't bring himself to even try it. I have tried it, on many occasions, and it is really tasty. Flavio is an expert at cooking it on the fireplace with the "*brace*", the embers from the log fire. When it is cooked to perfection (and marinated in a mixture of garlic and parsley), it is delicious. I wouldn't eat anything else.

So, I suppose it's not all bad stuff. Yes, there are the *zanzare*, the *calabrone* and so on, but I also experience foods over here that I would not otherwise have tried. And they're surprisingly not bad. And certainly, it's a change from having pie, beans and chips.

CHAPTER THIRTEEN

Cibo

I feel I need to dedicate an entire chapter to the food – *il cibo* – that makes up my daily life over here. There is no doubt in my mind that I eat much more healthily since moving to Sardinia compared to my life in Scotland. While I was never tempted by any of the stereotypical excesses that Scottish cuisine offers (Deep-fried Mars Bar anyone?), there is no denying that, generally speaking, we Scots (and I include myself here) do tend to eat a lot more heavy, carbohydrate-based foods than one might do compared to those living in the Mediterranean area.

It doesn't take a genius to work out why. The dreary, depressing climate in Scotland lends itself to a diet that offers some comfort to those suffering in the cold, wind and rain. Let's picture the scene: you've just come home after walking 15 minutes in the cold and rain, or you've managed to find a wee tea room while out on a walk somewhere when the wind and rain caught you unawares. What would you prefer? A bowl of salad and some fruit with an accompanying glass of fresh water, or a pie and a sausage roll followed by a steaming cup of tea and some cakes from the bakers. I know what I'd prefer, and I'm guessing that in a survey of 100 people, I wouldn't be in the minority.

Now picture instead that you've been out in Sardinia in July: it's roasting hot, you've been running from one place to another on various errands, you're sweating, and you finally get home. You are given the same choice as above. What do you go for this time? Well, those reading this who know me might well say that I'd still go for the tea, sausage roll and cakes, however, I can assure you I wouldn't, even if the baker's cakes did include an empire biscuit. I'd take the fresh water, fruit (preferably straight from the fridge) and salad every time. Thus, need I elucidate further: my diet has changed for the better since living here (and that's despite my 'occasional' trips to the bar in the morning – see Chapter 7).

The point is, I appreciate things over here that I never would have considered when living in Scotland. An example is something as simple as toasting some fresh bread on the *caminetto* (fireplace) and sprinkling it with some home-made extra-virgin olive oil. Absolutely delicious. We buy our olive oil from a colleague from Stefania's work who has his own olive groves (not uncommon over here), and makes the olive oil himself by taking his collection of olives to the *frantoio* - the olive-pressing machine. This gives him enough oil to get him through the whole year, as well as selling on to friends and colleagues. The oil is truly wonderful, and I now appreciate the difference between home-made olive oil like that and the one that you can find in a bottle in the supermarket for £3 a bottle. If you had told me 15 years ago that I would have become a connoisseur of olive oil and would be fussy about which to use, I'd have laughed in your face and politely told you not to talk such nonsense (or words to that effect ...).

A noticeable thing over here is the ubiquity of fruit at the dinner table at the end of the meal. I have not had a meal over here where fruit has not been offered. Moreover, most fruit tends to be bought locally, and therefore the fruit you eat depends on the season. At the moment, as I'm writing this, in Autumn and Winter, one of the main fruits of the season is oranges (and its cousins, such as mandarins and clementines). You can buy a kilo of oranges (that gives you around 5 or 6 oranges depending on their size) for as little as 50 cents depending on where you're buying them, but certainly for not more than €1. At current exchange rates that's about 6p an orange. You see locals selling the oranges that they've grown on their own land (and other fruit for that matter) from the side of the road, usually from the back of their *Ape,* or even from the front door of their house, marked by placing a couple of crates of oranges outside or using a home-made sign. They usually use these ancient, iron weighing scales to get the weight right, with the fruit on one side and the weighing masses on the other. I've not seen these instruments for decades. I love buying my fruit from these guys. Just don't ask for a receipt!

San Vito, and nearby Muravera, represent the home of the citrus fruits in Sardinia, where a huge proportion of the orange and lemon groves on the island can be found. It's possible to visit these orange and lemon groves during the *Sagra degli Agrumi,* the Citrus Festival that is held every April in Muravera. The Festival marks the end of the citrus fruit season and it is a major event in the local calendar. Because of Stefania's family ties in the area, we have been several times and it is a fantastic experience (see Chapter 25 – Sagra – for more details).

Visiting the orange and lemon groves themselves is wonderful enough – you can help yourself as you walk round, the proprietor insists upon it, as it saves them pruning the trees themselves at the end of the season. I must add here that the oranges are just amazing, so juicy and fragrant that it is hard to believe that the locals are of the opinion that the oranges at the end of the season are not quite as tasty as in the middle of the season, and in fact, some avoid buying at this time of the year for this reason. They should try the oranges I was used to buying in my local Fruitsco in Edinburgh. They'd have a bit of a fright, I'm sure.

I've said already that people over here are closer to *la terra* than anything I've ever experienced in my life, living in the UK (see Chapter 9). While not everyone will have an *orto* (an allotment), they will know someone who does, and more often than not, people will purchase a good proportion of their fruit and veg from their friend or relative that has an *orto*.

Recently a good friend of ours (a parent of one of Luca's classmates) lost his job. He had worked in the same factory for almost 20 years but, as a consequence of the economic crisis, the business had to enter into *cassa integrazione*, a strange phenomenon somewhere between a business working and not working that I have not quite fully understood yet so it's beyond me to provide a suitable explanation. Anyway, finally, after several months, the business collapsed completely, thus making Andrea, our friend, redundant.

Andrea (pronounced An-dray-a and not An-dree-a like the female name in English) is a man of means and someone I admire greatly. He didn't mope about and get depressed when he discovered he was redundant like a lot of people might do in his situation. With a colleague (well, an ex-colleague given that the factory had closed down), he decided to cultivate a piece of land that he had in the family, but that had been abandoned over the years, a few kilometres from Cagliari, in the countryside. With a lot of hard graft and no shortage of trials and tribulations along the way (the dry climate didn't help their task), the two men managed to turn the piece of land into an efficient, fully-operational *orto*, that provided them with the possibility of growing several different kinds of fruit and vegetables that would not only feed their respective families, but would also provide them with enough to be able to sell on to friends and relatives at a very reasonable price.

I went to visit Andrea one day to have a look at what his hard work had produced, and it was amazing. He showed me photographs of what the land looked like before they started cultivating it, and I was able to compare with what they had now. It was quite something - very impressive. There were tomatoes, aubergines, courgettes, lettuces, potatoes, green beans, as well as watermelons, oranges, pears and apples. I felt like I was visiting Gerard Depardieu on the set of *Jean de Florette*, only the difference was there was no Daniel Autueil there to sabotage his hard work. And unfortunately, no Emmanuelle Béart. Also, Andrea is not humpbacked. Apart from that, it was exactly the same.

We procure a lot of our fruit and veg from Andrea and, aside from the small savings we might make compared to supermarket prices, we are sure that the fruit and veg are not treated with pesticides and God knows whatever else, and that it's not been transported half-way round the world either. There's a big thing over here about fruit and veg being 0km (*"chilometro zero"*). There are signs everywhere advertising this fact in all the local *frutta e verdura* shops. They take a lot of pride in this. While it would be rather pedantic - and really rather annoying - of me to question the shop-owners on their 0km policy on the basis that, if the fruit and veg was really grown at 0km, surely that must mean there is an *orto* in the backshop, it does give a signal to the potential buyer that the fruit and veg has been grown locally, and that fact is highly valued over here.

There is probably one main reason over and above the more obvious ones (i.e. the organic nature of the produce and the desire to help the local economy) that will surely help in ensuring the survival of these local *frutta e verdura* shops when up against the fruit and veg that can be bought at the cheaper conglomerate supermarkets, and that's quite simply: the taste! There is no comparison in my eyes (or taste buds) between the fruit and veg you find in the supermarkets and the fruit and veg that you can buy at one of the 0km *frutta e verdura* shops. The produce of the 0km shops is significantly more tasty and delicious.

I still remember a few years ago when we had an English au-pair come to stay with us during the school holidays. She could not believe how tasty the watermelons were. She munched her way through about 37 huge watermelons in the four weeks she was with us (not that I was counting). But I knew exactly where she was coming from. When we first moved over here I was always saying, "Man, I've never tasted watermelons like that before. So that's what they're supposed to taste like". And I would say exactly the same thing about all the other fruits that we would find. In that phrase you could replace "watermelons" with "cherries", "oranges", "grapes" and even "pomegranates", as well as many other fruits, some of which I didn't even know existed before I moved here (remember, I'm from Kilmarnock, not Notting Hill).

For example, there are *fichi d'india*, which translates as prickly pears. Stefania thinks this translation is ridiculous, as they neither look or taste anything like pears - in fact, she was getting quite carried away one day about the whole matter, and launched into a full-scale discourse at the dinner table. It's not the *fichi d'india* that are the prickly ones, I thought to myself. Though I didn't have the courage to say it out loud. *Cachi*, or persimmons (however on a recent visit to London I saw these being sold at a greengrocer as *Kaki*) are such a bizarre kind of fruit. They have such a strange texture: very, very soft but incredibly sweet. I wasn't sure about these at first and just point blankly refused to eat them (I repeat, I'm from Kilmarnock, not Notting Hill). However, eventually I struck up the courage to try them and I do actually like them. After I started eating them Stefania decided to point out to me that one of these *cachi* has about the same calories as a twix, or something similar, as they are full of sugar. She always has to ruin it for me.

Anyway, whatever kind of fruit is eaten at the end, the kind of meal I described in Buon lavoro! (Chapter 11) has now become fairly habitual for me, after my first breath-taking experience in Dorgali with the head-teacher and her husband. Whether it's because we've decided to go somewhere nice for a meal, like an *agriturismo*, or whether we are celebrating something special, there is always a five course, lengthy meal on offer that will last for several hours. And it seems to me that there is something to celebrate over here almost on a weekly basis: it could be something religious (like Saint days, someone's first communion, or their confirmation, or even a wedding) or instead it might be someone's birthday, or simply because it's Sunday and it's important to get together, usually with one's family and 'celebrate' (Sunday is actually marked "*festa*" here on the calendar, meaning festival/celebration). But whatever it is that's being celebrated, it always revolves around the *cibo*, and *eating well*.

CHAPTER FOURTEEN

Bambini

For several months after we moved to Sardinia, while we were waiting for our new car to finally arrive off the production line (that's how it felt), I had to use public transport almost every day to get around Cagliari. And most of the time I was travelling with the children, either on the buses or on the "*metropolitano*". The buses can get really busy, but I was always struck by the willingness of others, sometimes young teenagers who in another context one might cross a street to avoid, to give up their seats in order to make my journey with the children that bit more easy and comfortable. I also remember an experience when a bus stopped for me while I was out with the children, and an elderly man, who was actually just passing the bus stop while out walking, stopped to help the kids get on the bus while I tried in vain to collapse the buggy in a time less than my usual protracted and uncoordinated 3 and a half minutes.

At the heart of these anecdotes is the oft-quoted, but certainly in my experience, completely accurate description of the Italians being a people who are extremely open and respectful towards young children (*bambini*). In my mind, there is no doubt about this aspect of Italian culture. Children are given an inordinate amount of attention by people in the street, who will bend down and talk to them, touch them, and generally show a level of interest in them that, if one were to behave similarly in the UK, you would probably end up in court accused of child molestation or undue and unwanted harassment towards strangers.

When going to a restaurant, young children are welcomed by the waiters and waitresses like royalty, given special dispensation and granted a particularly elevated level of patience and understanding. For example, in our personal experience, if one of your children happens to break some crockery or a glass, it is almost laughed off as if it is to be expected. Compare this to the same incident occurring in a British restaurant, especially after 8pm, and you would, more often than not, be scorned upon, not only for having "allowed" your child to break something, but also for having brought them into the restaurant in the first place ("What were you thinking? Don't you know that restaurants are not for children? Look at the time. Are you crazy?"). In fact, over here, I have been guilty on occasion of taking advantage of the high level of tolerance towards children by blaming almost everything on them, thus ensuring immunity from any blame being apportioned to me. "Oh, I'm sorry, but our youngest has just knocked over that beer glass again. Yes, I know, he's so clumsy".

I think that, on reflection, we do go out to restaurants with the kids much more over here than we ever did in Scotland, and during the summer months it's common to be out until midnight or later, where you can see little groups of children running about freely (I should add before you envisage a scene of wild children running in-between restaurant tables and chairs that it is usually the case that we are sitting outside and there is usually a play space or similar for the kids to run around). Of course, the reason that things do happen a lot later over here is that it is just too hot to go out in the warm summer months any time before 5.30pm, and often, especially if you are going out for a meal, you will go out much later than this.

The only problem is that when you are meeting others, you have to agree on an appointment time. It is generally felt that people from Mediterranean cultures are notoriously bad time-keepers, and despite my reluctance to generalise and stereotype again, I have to say that in my experience of living over here, there is a (fairly large) grain of truth in this. They even know it themselves. Recently, I had to park my car very close to the school gates at Anna's school (I usually just drop her off) as she needed help carrying some kind of artistic contraption she had made. The problem is that the traffic police are always around the school in the mornings as it is a notoriously busy spot and the traffic commonly gets 'stuck'. The policeman asked me what I was doing, and I replied that I was only going to be a minute. He then said, "*Ok, ma non un minuto all'italiana*" in a slightly aggressive tone. This basically means "If it is truly a minute then fine but not if you mean a minute *Italian style* (i.e. 10 minutes)".

When people say, "we'll meet you at the park at 6pm", I now know they actually mean nearer 7pm. It took me several months (and several lonely hours spent twiddling my thumbs) to finally work this out. When there is a birthday party for one of the friends of the kids and the time they write on the invitation is 5.30pm, Stefania has expressly warned me that we should not turn up any time before 6.30pm. And it's true. When we had Luca's birthday party the first year after we moved, it was more than an hour after the specified time before anyone turned up. I was getting worried. In the end, there was almost every one of his classmates at the party: some even arrived 2 hours after the time written on the invitation. When I suggested that day that it was just rude and ill-mannered to have a host waiting more than an hour before turning up at a party, Stefania just looked at me as if I was mad. She didn't even bother giving me a reply.

Another thing is that, over here, it is expected that the whole family comes to the birthday party – not just the celebrant's friend or schoolmate. Not so long ago we were invited to the 12th birthday party of one of Luca's schoolmates (a girl). All the families were invited. Parents, siblings, pets, grandparents. Just bring them along. We even had our au-pair staying with us at the time. We double-checked but it was no problem. We sat out in their *cortile* (courtyard) until well after midnight, enjoying the *cibo* and drinks while the kids played away in another part of the house.

When I think now of how kids' birthday parties tended to be organised in the UK, the contrast is striking. I still remember some of Luca's birthday parties when we were living in Scotland (and those of his friends) where a hall, a softplay area or similar would be hired for a specified 90-minute period and the invitation would have written: "from 4.30-6pm". And they meant it. At 6pm you were shuffled out the door as quickly as you could say "where's my party bag?" as the next party attendees were being heralded in for the next "session". If you invited only Italians they'd only be at the party for the last 20 minutes or so. And if you brought along the whole family with you,

you'd probably be refused entry. "No, sorry there's a restricted quota we have to keep to – yes, for health and safety reasons. Only the children please. I'm sorry".

But, there's another thing over here with regard to birthdays: no party bags! Brilliant! What a result. No need to faff about with silly little bags, and stuff them with things that will hardly get a glance from the festive-goers as they traipse out the door. As a parent, I've often wondered about this whole party bag thing, as I certainly don't remember it being a concept when I was growing up. I do remember taking away from parties (and offering at mine) a piece of birthday cake, but I certainly do not recall giving away a bag with a yo-yo, a whistle and some penny chews. Although I believe the gifts in party bags are getting even more sophisticated (or expensive) these days. You begin to think, "whose birthday is it exactly?". Oh well, times have changed, but maybe not over here in Sardinia (well, not yet at least).

Anyway, people are always late over here, and you just have to accept it as part of the culture and try not to get too annoyed by it. However, the concept of being late took on an entirely new significance for us four months after we moved when Stefania announced to me that she was *"in ritardo"*. My reaction to this news of "lateness" was just as emotional as my reaction to people's continued lateness over here, only this time it was more one of joy, wonder and anticipation rather than frustration, anger and bewilderment.

I had never thought of the origin of the word "news" in English until I learned the word in Italian. For some reason (pass me that hat with the big 'D') I hadn't associated the word "news" with "something new", but in fact, in Italian they use the singular "new" (*novità*) to refer to news and usually associate it with something "beautiful" (*bella*). When we discovered that Stefania was pregnant, we were able to share our "*bella novità*" with family and friends.

Stefania had always said to me that the one thing she dreaded about being pregnant over here in Sardinia was the medicalisation of pregnancy care, as compared to going through a pregnancy in the UK. The number of checks she had to attend for various things during the pregnancy was unbelievable. In the UK, she had a scan at 20 weeks and a couple of visits to the midwife. Over here, we had a scan practically every couple of weeks with the constant presence of the gynaecologist and several visits with the midwife.

It is common practice in Italy to know in advance the sex of your baby, simply because it's difficult not to notice when you're going through all the scans. We decided we didn't want to know the sex until the baby was born, as that was what we had done with the other two, but it was difficult as we had to always remind the midwife and the gynaecologist not to refer to 'he' or 'she' when talking to us at our fortnightly scans.

Keeping the sex of the baby a mystery created a bit of a storm. People didn't believe us when we told them we didn't know the sex. "You mean you don't want to tell us. I understand." "No", we replied, "we actually don't know ourselves". This usually received a response of *"Macché!"* or *"Ma non scherzare"*, which both roughly translate as "Come on! Give us a break! You're having us on". And when we insisted that we really didn't know, they thought we were mad. "Why don't you want to know?" We usually replied along the lines of "It'll spoil the surprise". We didn't know before the births of Luca and Anna and it was a wonderful surprise to finally discover the sex just as they're born. A *bella novità*, as it were.

One of Stefania's friends recently gave birth to a little girl, Erica. We knew it was a girl several months prior to the birth. We even knew the name. The other day Stefania said to me "Erica's been born". I just kind of shrugged and said "Oh, right". There was no surprise. No news. Other than the fact that the mother and baby were both all right of course, not insignificant in itself, but nevertheless, I just felt there was no *"novità"* about it. It wasn't something *"new"*.

I still remember when I broke the *bella novità* of Stefania's pregnancy to Signor and Signora Rossi, our landlords. I think they must have known something as I was asked the leading question, "Have you got anything to tell us? Anything new?" when I was in paying the monthly rent. I would enter their house every month to hand over the rent – not in any way a wrench given they lived downstairs from us and almost always offered me a coffee and a chocolate and some interesting and friendly conversation to boot. On this occasion, however, Signor Rossi felt the occasion was worthy of opening something a bit stronger. I think he had it on ice waiting for me to come in. They were both genuinely delighted for us and were getting just as excited about the impending arrival to the "house" (as they put it) as we were, almost inferring we were all living together in one big family home. They went on to say that there hadn't been a new arrival in the street since Martina, their daughter was born almost 16 years ago.

We were fairly relaxed about the whole event and it seemed that everyone around us was much more excited than we were. The ladies who work in the pharmacy, the woman from the *panificio* (bread shop, not a baker - the difference will be explained later in Chapter 28) and the Signori who sell us our newspaper from the *edicola* (newspaper stand) from the corner of our street. Not to mention of course Stefania's parents, her relatives and her friends and colleagues.

We were constantly inundated with questions and they increased in frequency as we got closer to the due date… "How is the Signora? *Tutto bene*? (is everything ok?) Has she felt anything yet? When is the due date exactly? Surely it must be close now? Were your other two overdue? By how many days?" and so on and so on. My responses to these questions usually resulted in the questioner then confidently estimating when the baby would be born and what the sex would be. They couldn't all be right, so I just nodded my head and smiled, and then bade them farewell, promising I'd let them know if anything happened.

I seriously considered putting an advert in the local press or an announcement on the local radio when the baby arrived as I knew I wouldn't have the time to go around all the shops and bars to let them all know personally. While I did experience a degree of interest in the birth of my first two children from my family and even beyond, it never quite stretched to being the "big news" of the local community. I've sat and pondered about this. I think it's partly because, as I said at the beginning, that in Italy there does seem to be more interest in children generally, and they are given a special dispensation that I don't think one could ever argue is similar in the UK, or perhaps elsewhere for that matter. And secondly, it is certainly true that there are significantly fewer births in Italy per head of population than in most other European countries (although Italy is interestingly beaten into third place by Germany and Portugal for least number of births per head of population), and therefore it is a greatly anticipated event. Either way, it was nice to be popular, even if it was only for a few months.

CHAPTER FIFTEEN

Il presepe

The 8th of December is a national holiday over here. It celebrates the Immaculate Conception. I still remember suggesting to Stefania (at the risk of being pedantic and getting a slap) that, if this was the day when Mary was visited by a band of angels and discovered she was going to be having a baby in just over two weeks, do you not think there might have been some other indication by this point? Of course, I should have kept quiet. My ignorance on these matters is legendary. For those just as ignorant as me, the day doesn't celebrate the conception of Jesus Christ but instead the conception of the Blessed Virgin Mary in the womb of her mother. There you go. Now you know. Impress your friends and colleagues with that one.

Anyway, resisting the temptation to be pedantic again (i.e. depending on when she was born my original question still holds), I decided to keep quiet. Why should I question having a day off work and spending the entire day with my family, feasting on some lovely *cibo* and delicious wine? I found myself writing a text message to my mum the other day: "hopefully catch up with you tomorrow as it's the Immaculate Conception, so we'll be around all day". Brilliant. I never thought I'd ever include the words "Immaculate Conception" in a text message to my mum.

The day of the Immaculate Conception involves the usual festive aspects: getting together with the family (i.e. my in-laws) and eating and drinking all day. But the 8th December is also reserved for putting up the Christmas tree and the careful construction of the *presepe* (nativity scene). The *presepe* is an essential component of the Christmas decorations over here and is taken quite seriously. The fact they even have a specific word for it says enough.

Some families go all out on building up their *presepe* and make elaborate structures involving not only the main characters (the wise men, shepherds, the animals in the stable and of course Mary, Joseph and the baby Jesus) but also running water, spotlights and moving figures. You don't believe me? It's absolutely true. It is mandatory over here to have a nativity scene set up in your house for Christmas. If you want to put up a tree as well, fine, but don't even think of overlooking the *presepe*.

When I was growing up in Scotland, it was quite the opposite (in fact, still is, as far as I'm aware): in other words, absolutely everyone had a tree and tinsel, very few made the effort of making up a nativity scene. In fact, those that decided to elaborate on making a special effort with their decorations usually stretched to putting Christmas lights up in the garden or purchasing a flashy Santa that looked as if he was climbing up the drainpipe.

Each church will invest a lot of time and money making a particularly sophisticated *presepe* that will often attract visitors from all over the city who've heard that the Church of Saint Mary (for example) has a particularly amazing nativity scene. In fact, if you are ever visiting Cagliari at Christmas time I strongly recommend the *presepe* at the *Chiesa di Sant' Ignazio* near the Roman amphitheatre. It is truly incredible - like nothing you've ever seen before.

A few years ago, in Muravera, a tourist town close to San Vito where Stefania's family are originally from, there was a "treasure hunt" of around 20 different *presepe* that involved going from one location to another to admire the various nativity scenes that had been created by the local churches, businesses and even the local people that wanted to take part and had built a particularly impressive *presepe* in their front garden. We walked from one *presepe* to the next almost like a religious form of orienteering. There was a lovely atmosphere as we bumped into the same people as we made our way around the '*presepe* trail' exchanging notes on where the next one on the list could be found.

That same year we were staying in San Vito for Christmas and we ended up at midnight mass at the local town church. The church was packed full and the music was beautiful (mainly thanks to Stefania's cousins, Alessia and Giovanna, who organise the choir and the music group). When we all traipsed out of the church at the end of mass, at around 1 o'clock in the morning, people gathered in the little piazza, directly outside the church, where *spumante* (sweet fizzy wine) and *panettone* (sweet fruit bread, traditionally eaten in Italy at Christmas, as I'm sure you will all know) were waiting on trestle tables for the populace as they exchanged Christmas wishes. It was lovely, and it seemed that the whole village was in attendance. There was an amazing atmosphere, one of togetherness and community spirit.

Yes, Italy still appears on the surface very much a Catholic country. Or at least Sardinia does. The number of public holidays celebrated here is unbelievable, and they are almost always linked to religious feasts and Saint days. Other than the usual Christmas and Easter breaks, here we have the Immaculate Conception (obviously), Ferragosto

(15th August), All Saints Day (1st November), and the Saint of the town where you live. In Cagliari we have two: we have Saint Efisio's day ("*la festa di Sant'Efisio*") on 1st May, which is a religious festival, marked by a huge procession through the city where people dress up in traditional costume (to be described in more detail in Chapter 25 – Sagra). Then there is the Saint Saturnino day on the 30th October, which is to celebrate the patron saint of the city.

Aside from the obvious pleasure there is in having a day off work, there is something rather pleasant about actually having a meaning to the day's holiday. It is something that has been discussed in recent times in the UK, for example, there was some talk at one stage of having a British Day, and in Scotland, the Scottish Nationalist Party have been campaigning for a while to get St Andrew's Day recognised as a national public holiday.

In fact, when we lived in Scotland, Stefania often had a go at me (as if it was really all my fault) about the public holidays in the UK – not only for the lack of them, but the lack of meaning behind them. Bearing in mind that Italians also have a day off to mark when Italy became a republic and also, when they were liberated from Nazi oppression during the Second World War, she put it more or less like this, "in Italy we celebrate religious and significant historical national events, however, in Britain you celebrate when the banks have decided to close for a day". Ouch!

The good points about this include the comparative lack of commercialisation surrounding religious festivals, such as Christmas and Easter. And, in my opinion, this is particularly noticeable at this time of year. For example, as we approach the last nine days before Christmas, the churches are packed with people participating in the "*Novena*", where Christmas prayers and hymns are sung in a 30-minute service every day for the last nine days leading up to Christmas Day.

Christmas Day itself involves mostly eating and talking, and a lot less drinking and actual gift-exchanging than in my experience in the UK. Traditionally gifts were given to children on the Epiphany over here, that is, the 6th January, however, this is now beginning to change to doing it on Christmas Day or Christmas Eve, in line with many other countries in the Western World (perhaps with the exception of Spain). However, on the Epiphany (6th January) there is still the tradition of children putting up their stocking the night before for it to be filled by the "*Befana*" (Witch), who will leave sweets and chocolates for the children who have been good all year, and coal for those who have been naughty.

The similarities between the cultural 'role' of Santa Claus and the *Befana* are obvious, however, the lines between the two are now being blurred somewhat in Italy by the increasing use of "*Babbo Natale*" in addition to the *Befana* around Christmas time. Although interestingly, the use of *Babbo Natale* does not include leaving the stocking the night before Christmas. This special role of hosiery replenishment has been reserved for the *Befana* still. Which does cause a degree of confusion in our bi-cultural family, however. The kids expect their stockings to be filled by Santa on Christmas Day and then again by the *Befana* on the 6th January. They haven't had the nerve to question this clear overlapping of roles in too much detail yet. I think they know that, by doing so, it might unravel a lot of things that they might not want to hear. Best to keep quiet and take advantage of the double quantities of sweeties (or in our case: a toothbrush, a tangerine and a €2 coin, amongst other tat).

The beauty of Christmas over here (or not, depending on your view) is that on Boxing Day, "*il giorno di Santo Stefano*" (St Stephen's Day), means that you get to do it all over again. It's a bit like "Christmas Day – the sequel": everyone gets together again, having another huge, drawn-out meal, and basically enjoying each other's company over the dinner table. This can be a problem, however, if you offer to "host" Christmas, since it means you will have the family for Christmas Eve dinner (which is also a big event), all day Christmas Day, and then again, all day on Boxing Day.

This coming year as I write this will be a particularly laborious time to be hosting Christmas since Christmas Day will fall on the Friday, and with Boxing Day on the Saturday, it means that on the 27th December, which will be a Sunday, everyone will get together again as a family, as it's traditional here to celebrate a Sunday together with a long drawn out meal too. So, the Christmas eating and hosting will last three full days (that's why we're escaping to Kilmarnock to spend Christmas this year). In comparison, the idea of 'hosting' Christmas UK style - i.e. for a few hours for Christmas dinner - doesn't seem quite such a daunting prospect anymore. And you don't even have to trouble yourself with constructing a *presepe* either, unless you really want to. But if you do, just make sure it's an intricately complex one, otherwise it might be sniffed at.

CHAPTER SIXTEEN

Tradizioni

The Italians have an expression that is usually used at weddings to wish the happy couple all the best, "*auguri e figli maschi*", which translates roughly as "best wishes and hope you have male children". Beyond the clearly sexist and chauvinistic overtones, as well as it being just a horrible anachronism in the modern age (although Stefania, perhaps in trying to defend her countrymen - and countrywomen - has just said to me that she hasn't heard the expression in years. I disagree. I still hear it), I was always really puzzled by this. How could one not want a beautiful wee girl, a loving daughter, just as much as a little boy? As the due date approached for the birth of our third child, I was getting more and more excited, and the truth was, I would have been equally delighted whether it was a boy or a girl.

It was early February, just over a year after we moved, and I was rushing to the hospital as quickly as I could, abandoning my usual careful, considerate driving style in order to avoid a calamitous and disastrous situation. The baby was coming!

Stefania was desperate to have the birth in water, in the birthing pool, as she did with the other two, however, on this occasion there wasn't even the time to fill the pool with water. The baby was wasting no time in arriving. It was a boy! A beautiful wee baby boy! I was instructed to go out and buy a blue ribbon and attach it to the outside of our front door, thus proclaiming to the world (well, our neighbours in the street) that we had had a boy. So, I didn't need to place an advert in the local paper after all. There was a system already in place for such an announcement. Of course, had it been a girl, I would have had to have stuck a pink ribbon to the door. Who said that they can be rather traditional over here???

We named him Finn – a British (Celtic) name to balance out the fact that he was born here and continuing our trend of giving a name to our child from the "other" country from where the baby was born. We also continued our trend of giving our children only 4 letters to their names, a fact not overlooked by some of our friends and relatives.

"Fraser, what are you so worried about. We don't tax on the length of the names over here you know", said Flavio. Well, they tax just about everything bloody else, I replied.

The joy in Finn arriving was slightly moderated by a typical Italian saga that ensued on the day we went to register his birth at the *Comune* (Town Hall) Registry office. We wanted to name our new addition to the Lauchlan family, 'Finn Mancini Lauchlan'. Mancini is Stefania's surname and we had already included it as a middle name for our eldest two children, though as they were born (and their births were registered) in Scotland, we never came up against any problem with this decision. Indeed, I would say that it is quite common to have your mother's maiden name as a middle name in Scotland (my own middle name is my mother's maiden name, and I know plenty of others that follow that same rule). In fact, one may even argue further and say it is almost a tradition to do so, thus carrying forward the mother's surname as well as the father's.

When we declared that we wished to have Mancini as Finn's middle name we got a few 'hums' and 'haws' and a few pregnant pauses from the first Registrar at the *Comune*. Not a no, but certainly some feeling of doubt that this was 'legal'. She actually printed off the papers for us to sign, but then her boss - a short, plump, pompous asshole of a man[2] - entered the room, and unfortunately for us, the lady Registrar decided to check things out with him. With this decision she didn't realise that she was thus triggering a saga that was to include court appearances and legal wrangles that were to go on for approximately another two and a half years.

I'll try and be concise, otherwise I could write a hell of a lot more. The issue is thus: in Italy, there is no understanding of the concept of a 'middle name'. There are forenames (in fact, most often usually only one forename) and surnames (again, most often, only one surname). There are some instances of two surnames that I know of, but it is certainly uncommon, and it would be the equivalent of the British notion of a double-barrelled surname, not as a middle name and a surname. I do know of more people over here who have two forenames (though it is not that common a thing either), however, the two forenames are usually said together as if it is one long forename (similarly as is used in the UK, especially of female Catholic names, for example, Maria Elisabetta, Anna Chiara or Anna Maria, and so on).

The short, fat, pompous one's argument was this: there is no such concept as a middle name in Italy, thus, you cannot have a surname (Mancini) as one of the forenames for your child. We argued

---

[2] Note that this description of the town council employee involved has been changed to ensure anonymity. If his lawyers are reading this I can confirm that he was not like this at all.

with him that this would mean that our 3rd child would be different from the other two, who already have their mother's surname as part of their name. However, this just added fuel to his fire, and he retorted that this should never have been allowed. When we explained that they were born in Scotland, he argued that when we moved over here to live, we should have been told by the appropriate authorities to change our children's names - a preposterous argument.

Thus, he added, not only would he refuse to allow us to name our child as Finn Mancini Lauchlan, but moreover, he would be writing to the Italian equivalent of the Procurator Fiscal to investigate the matter of two children who were living in Italy who had a surname as a forename (a most outrageous and serious criminal act it seemed). When I pointed out that I was living in Italy and I had a surname as a forename (according to the strict boundaries of Italian forenames and surnames and no middle names), he just ignored me. I don't know why I wasn't considered important enough to be investigated for the same criminal act that my children were being accused of, but there you go. Part of me, a big part of me, felt that we were the victims of a stuck-up, power-hungry, probably sexually repressed, jobsworth, who also had a slightly sinister xenophobic undercurrent to him[3]. Were we being picked on here simply because we, or more accurately, I was not Italian? I can only guess but that was my feeling on it.

We discovered afterwards that he had no right to refuse to grant us our chosen name for our child, but rather he should have warned us that, in his professional view, our chosen name may not be considered legal and that there may be a case to answer. But we didn't know that at the time. Thus, after further arguments with him, we had to eventually relent, and instead we decided to name our child Finn Bernardo Lauchlan. The short, fat, pompous one was in front of his computer when we announced our amended name.

I wish I had had a camera with me to take a picture of his facial expression. It would have been framed and shown to all those who came across his pomposity to savour. "Ah, I see what you're doing", he stated, as he was clearly scanning through all our family demographic information on his computer. But there was nothing he could do. Bernardo, a valid forename, and therefore with which he could take no exception at all, was Stefania's mother's surname, and so we were able to sneak in a wee reference to Stefania's side of the family after all. Bernardo can be a surname as well as a forename, just like many other names in Italy:

---

[3] Again, please note that this description has been changed in order to ensure anonymity of the very nice town council employee.

Valentino, Franco, Simone, Costantino, Marcello, to name just a few, which really renders the whole argument of 'surnames cannot be forenames' rather meaningless.

Stefania received a phone call several months after we had registered Finn's birth from the regional court to say that they had received a report from a council employee on the use of surnames as forenames for our two eldest children. The clerk of the court who called was almost apologetic as she informed us that they had to follow the report up by having an open case on it.

Several months later we had to attend court to 'defend ourselves'. It was ludicrous. I just kept thinking of the waste of public money that was spent on everyone's time to follow this through. We had to sit in court and discuss the Scottish tradition of using your mother's surname as a middle name (it perhaps could be argued that I indulged in a little hyperbole during my defence: I think I mentioned the clan system at one point and the importance of maintaining family lineage for such important things as the correct tartan that should be used in ceremonial dress. All rubbish of course). Anyway, the end result: we won. We didn't have to change Luca and Anna's names at all. At least common sense did eventually prevail in amongst all the bureaucratic nonsense.

However, this wasn't the only time that I have come up against anachronistic, bureaucratic nonsense since moving here. The day that we went to the *Comune* to register my residency (residency is taken much more seriously over here than back home), Stefania had to come with me. She had to sign something confirming that I was living in the house with her. Not only that, for my residency to go ahead I had to provide evidence that I had a job here in Italy, or else that I had at least €5000 in the bank. I didn't have a job at this point, but regardless, I found it remarkable and an unnecessary invasion of privacy to have to prove that I had more than €5000 in the bank.

My protestations that the UK was an EU country, and therefore I had every right to live here regardless of my employment status or wealth, fell on deaf ears (please note that this happened several years before *Brexit*). Further arguments regarding the fact that my wife and (at the time) two children lived here also were not given any consideration, so in the end I had to provide confirmatory evidence of my (very moderate) wealth. I've learned by now that there is no use arguing with these people who work in these bureaucratic positions. Once they've made their mind up about what is required, they will not be swayed (unless you offer some kind of 'incentive', allegedly). I decided just to go ahead and produce what was required for this particular signora, since, as Stefania quipped, we might come back another day and be told that we cannot change my residency without a formal blessing from the Pope.

Aside from the fact that this involved more

time-wasting in returning home to find a bank statement and returning to the *Comune,* I did think this was inherently ridiculous. If I were unable to provide such evidence, did this mean that I was not allowed to live with my own wife and children? I wondered aloud if such restrictions would be placed on a situation where the roles were reversed, i.e. the Italian was the husband in a full-time job and the British wife was applying for Italian residency. I may be wrong, but perhaps this scenario would not have been met with such resistance. It is reflective of the very traditional (and some might say, deeply anachronistic) values that still exist over here.

CHAPTER SEVENTEEN

The verde verde grass of home

The Italians have a very similar expression to us, *"l'erba del vicino è sempre più verde"* (literally, "the neighbour's grass is always greener"). I'm always struck by how many people over here say to me "You're from Scotland? What are you doing living here? Scotland is beautiful. I would love to live in Scotland". Of course, this situation is mirrored when I'm back in Scotland on holidays and I receive frequent envious remarks about the life I must be leading in Sardinia. I've lost count of the number times I've had to endure the "you lucky so and so" comment from friends and family. Only they don't say "so and so".

It's not difficult to provide an explanation for

these two seemingly contrasting views, over and above the use of the proverb of the grass always being greener. There is perhaps, certainly amongst some people, the mistaken view that there exists some kind of paradise on Earth, a land where everything is perfect and wonderful. Of course, we could perhaps argue that there are some places in this world that are better than others, but that doesn't mean that these 'better' places have everything. As far as I'm concerned, every place has its advantages and disadvantages. And, moreover, I think that there are aspects to one place (let's say, Scotland) that may be considered disadvantages by those living in that place at that time, but those same aspects are looked on enviously by others living in an entirely different environment (let's say, Sardinia). Let me explain.

The first Christmas after we moved we had a bit of seasonal heat wave, with unusual temperatures, even hitting as high as 26oC (approximately 80oF), while at the same time, my friends and family were bemoaning the exceptionally cold winter they were enduring in Scotland and were expressing their envy to me fairly belligerently via telephone or email. However, there was a bit of me (actually a large part of me) that was envious of *them* and the snowy, wintry weather they were having back home, including a white Christmas that year. The weather in Sardinia at Christmas, while pleasantly warm, just didn't feel right to me. I felt I was being cheated somehow. I shouldn't be going out wearing short sleeves at Christmas – it's just not cricket!

I'm sure there may well be some who will think I'm crazy thinking this, but maybe not. And this has not been the only occasion where I've experienced a 'weak moment' (read 'huge dollop of homesickness') since we moved. Other occasions include every time I have to go to the post office or the bank where the execution of the simplest transaction or postal service takes an inordinate amount of time. When Stefania's rushing out the door on her way to work and asks if I could go to the post office for her, my whole being just collapses into depression as I know all the plans I've made for that morning must be put to the side. The slow, arduous process of bureaucracy just drives me round the bend, to the point where I feel I've turned the bend and I'm on my way back to where I started. Indeed, this occurs frequently – you get sent from one office to another to get some document or other that you were supposed to bring and eventually you return to the point where you were 2 or 3 hours ago. It's no wonder that my experiences of *'deja-vu'* have increased exponentially since moving here.

The other occasions when I get homesick are perhaps more understandable, and will be especially so for those who have ever moved away to a place far away from where they grew up. I'm talking of the times when you just miss, and I mean really, really miss, your family and friends, people you've known all your life and who know you inside out, and with whom you can just sit down, usually over the ubiquitous cup of tea or pint, and just talk freely in your own language or dialect, about anything or anyone. Included within this is an aspect of Scottish life that I miss terribly – a bit of banter. And I don't mean the kind of "Glesga banter" satirised brilliantly by Ford Kiernan and Greg Hempill in the BBC Scotland comedy sketch show 'Chewin' the Fat'. I just mean the kind of relaxed, jokey conversation you usually have with anyone – your friends, your family, even strangers at a bus stop – that immediately puts a smile on your face. Even if it's pelting down with rain while you're waiting for the bus to come.

However, I digress. To return to my original point, there are many people over here, perhaps surprisingly, who look at me quizzically when I say I moved here from Scotland. That is, apart from my brother-in-law, Flavio.

Flavio is a fantastic guy, and has become somewhat of a soulmate and best friend for me over here. We've known each other ever since I first came over to Sardinia for visits with Stefania, more than 20 years ago. Now that he's married to Stefania's sister, Sara, we have become relatives, however, our friendship goes beyond any family ties. After Stefania, he's the guy I turn to if there's anything I want to talk about. He is also talented with practical things – anything that requires hands-on work - and, on more than several occasions than I'd care to count, has come to my rescue with anything from fixing the kids electrical toys to building up flat-packed furniture to being a part-time mechanic for our car. If I have a problem, Flavio will fix it for me. He's basically a real, true-to-life version of Bob the Builder. And when one has inherited a clumsiness gene, and has major problems with basic spatial orientation, having someone like Flavio around is a God-send.

We play football twice a week, sometimes go to the Cagliari games together at the stadium, and often go out for a pint. Flavio made the effort, right from the very first time we met, to make me feel welcome as a stranger in a foreign land. There was no initial suspicion or fear that I was from another country (a feeling that I still encounter over here, even though I'm now fluent in the language, married to a Sardinian and with 'Sardinian' children). Flavio has always treated me as he would treat anyone else that he considered to be a close friend – which usually involves taking the piss out of me, as I do to him. These exchanges with Flavio are probably the closest I get to experiencing a bit of the 'Glesga banter'. If I didn't have Flavio, the truth is I would probably feel a bit lost and isolated over here.

Flavio is the one person who has never said to me, "Why did you move over here?". In fact, he was genuinely puzzled as to why it took us so long to actually make the move 'back' to Sardinia. To Flavio, living in Sardinia is almost like living on paradise, and he's always quick to point out the virtues of living here rather than the downsides.

One of the main things for which I'm indebted to Flavio is the fact that he was able to integrate me into the twice-weekly football game with his friends. Right from the first week we arrived in Sardinia he made sure I'd get a game. I've always enjoyed my football - more so playing than watching - and the thought that I might not be able to play on a frequent basis when we moved to Italy filled me with dread. I was relieved that Flavio managed to ensure my place in the footballing group as quickly as he did. I've been playing with the same group of friends now for several years and I've got to know them all very well. It took them a while to learn my name ("Fritz", "Fresh", and the good old "Freezer" are just some of the misnomers), and indeed some of them still mispronounce it to this day, several years on, however, this doesn't bother me. I'm like the exotic mascot for the group - *lo scozzese*. I also find myself in situations with the group that I can never imagine finding myself in with my old footballing friends back in Scotland.

The week after Finn was born I turned up at the football park for our usual Monday evening match. By this time, I had been playing with the same guys for over a year. We had even been out a few times for a pizza. However, I wouldn't quite have said by this point that we were really close friends. Despite this, they lined up one after one to kiss me on both cheeks to congratulate me on the birth of my third child. Flavio had told them the reason why I was unable to play the previous week and they all felt the need to mark the event by giving me a kiss and wishing me all the best. I can't quite imagine the same scenario playing itself out on any of the football parks around Britain. If you tried to do something similar, you would probably end up with a right hook to your jaw. Usually I would greet my fellow teammates in Scotland with a grunt when I entered the field of play and a grunt at the end, though always, strangely enough, with a handshake when the final whistle blows – a tradition, I've noticed, that is not always extended to your adversaries over here.

The only other information you may share with your fellow 5-a-side teammates in Scotland is whether you are able or not to make it the following week. I still recall one of the lads I used to play with in Edinburgh announcing that he couldn't make it the following week as he was getting married and he'd be away to the Maldives on his honeymoon. No-one even knew Tam was engaged, let alone getting married. The response from his footballing mates, with whom he'd been meeting up and playing football with every week for several years, was not to offer heartfelt congratulations to him, wishing him all the best in his impending marriage (God forbid demonstrating any warmth in a physical way: a hug or a kiss? you must be joking), but instead it was to enquire in an ever-so-slightly aggressive tone, "So will you make it the week after, then?"

Instead, in Italy, after playing football every week for several years, I would say that I know my fellow teammates fairly well – sometimes too well. I'm not referring to the kissing – I no longer wince at the thought of kissing another man – it's now a common part of my everyday activity over here. I'm referring instead to the rather bizarre conversations I find myself having with my teammates that I know for sure would never occur if I were still in Scotland.

A bit of context is required here before I launch into this next story, and that involves discussing that most wonderful French invention that you can even now find in many bathrooms around the UK (well, not in THAT many): *the bidet*. Despite it being French, the bidet is quintessentially Italian: apparently Italy is the number 1 country in the world for the bidet, where it can be found in 97% of households.

I must be honest here: before moving to Italy I really was unsure what the whole point of the bidet was. My knowledge did stretch to know that it was not for washing your feet but instead to wash the more intimate parts of one's body (though I was approximately 23 years old when I discovered this), but more than that, I was fairly ignorant. My defence is that I did not experience many bidets in the homes and properties that I frequented as a lad growing up in Kilmarnock in the 1970s and 80s.

Probably not an experience that was unique to me either.

The first dilemma that you face when using a bidet is: which way do you face? It took me years before I had the courage to actually ask someone (the correct response being towards the taps, just in case you didn't know). At the beginning I was rather distrustful, or wary, of the bidet for some reason – I just didn't feel comfortable about the thought of using it, and so avoided it. However, after some months of living in our new apartment I felt I just couldn't ignore the bidet any longer. It was like this big, white elephant staring back at me every time I went in to use the amenities. I tentatively tried it one day – and what bliss. It was fantastic. I felt so refreshed without having to take a full bath or a shower. Now I don't know what I'd do without one – not something I readily admit to my dear friends back in Scotland. I'm sure you can imagine the response I'd get if I did.

Now, what has the bidet got to do with my footballing friends? Well, after a match one Monday in August, we were engaging in our usual after-match conversation and I was keen to ask one of my team-mates how his holiday had gone. He was visiting London and had never been before. "Oh, it was a nightmare", replied Fabrizio. "Oh? Why was that? Did you not go to any of the sights: Tower Bridge, Big Ben, the Houses of Parliament, The British Museum", I enquired, slightly bewildered by his negative response, as most people who visit London for the first time are bowled over by the experience. "Oh, yes, we did all that, but it was where we were staying. It was a nice hotel and all that, but there was no bidet".

I must have looked at Fabrizio a bit strangely at this point, wondering to myself: how could not having a bidet ruin someone's holiday? He continued, "I mean every time I had a shite, I had to go into the shower. It was terrible". I just looked at him stunned. Of course, my immediate thought was to reply along the lines of, "could you not just have wiped your arse and got on with it?", but the correct words in Italian didn't immediately come to me, as I was trying so hard to stifle a chuckle. I was imagining the impossibility of having a similar conversation with one of my footballing pals back in Scotland:

Me: "So how was your honeymoon then, Tam?"

Tam: "Oh well, it was alright. I mean the Maldives is some place and aw that, but you know something? There wasn't even a fucking bidet in the hotel room".

Me: "Aw, you're joking. That must have been hellish. How did you cope?"

Tam: "Well, no' very well really. It just ruined it for me, you know. Just ruined it. I'll no be back".

That bizarre conversation with Fabrizio made me reflect though. The grass may always be greener on the other side, and it may be nice to go there for a visit and see what beautiful things are there. But, the other side may be lacking in some things that you're used to and comfortable with, regardless of how beautiful and green the neighbour's grass is. What if you actually like the colour of grass on your own side, despite its faults? I'm still working out which side of the garden fence I'm living on. Scotland is beautiful, and I do miss it sometimes. But I'm used to my bidet now and there's not many bidets kicking about in Scotland.

CHAPTER EIGHTEEN

Graffiti

If there is one thing that I get annoyed about over here (well, apart from the *zanzare*, the endless bureaucracy, the dangerous driving, the tardiness of the locals, the anachronistic values and I'll just add in here the lack of decent infrastructure), it's the amount of graffiti. It's everywhere and is a total eyesore, a blot on the landscape. It seems to me that the locals are now immune to it and don't seem to notice it the same way I do. It's virtually impossible to find a street that doesn't have some degree of vandalism sprayed on its walls or buildings.

After Finn was born, we had to start looking for a new house. We had grown out of our 2-

bedroomed apartment, above Signor and Signora Rossi. There was no longer enough space for the five of us. The problem was each time we went to look at a new house I would turn to Stefania and say, "But look at the graffiti – I don't think I like this area", as my Scottish mind was making a direct connection with the amount of graffiti and the desirability of the area. However, there is so much graffiti over here that the locals don't seem to make such a connection. Indeed, Stefania responded by saying that, if I didn't want to buy a house where there's graffiti within 100 yards of the house, then we would need to move out to the country. And, unfortunately, she's right. When I say it's everywhere, I mean it: it's everywhere. Even the kids notice it.

Not long after we moved, we were in the car and Luca had his eyes fixed on some building that had been spray painted with several messages - some interesting and political, others not so – and asked: "why do they do that Daddy? That's not nice", as if it was the first time he had seen graffiti in his life. Just as I was about to embark on a long and philosophical discourse about the rights and wrongs of vandalising various kinds of property, my 3-year old daughter pipes up: "Maybe they've run out of paper, Daddy". Well, that's one way of looking at it.

The messages do range from the outright offensive to the political to the intimately personal (usually declarations of love and the like).

However, I am impressed by some of the political messages strewn all over some of the buildings, many of which relate to communism and Marxist politics for some reason. For example, the other day I saw one that said: "the 21st Century will mark the springtime of Marx and Engels" – you won't get that written on many walls around Kilmarnock. Another one I see close to where we live is: "*Se hai il cuore a sinistra non tenere il portafoglio a destra*", which translates more or less as "If your heart leans to the left, don't invest your money as one would who's from the right". I really like that one. Because of the economic crisis over here (and in many other parts of the world it should be said) there are many cuts being made to public services, and a lot of them are being made in education. Outside one school I saw a creative piece of graffiti that said simply: "Itaglia", which would be pronounced the same as "Italia", only the word "taglia" means "cut". Ingenious.

Of course, there are some political messages of graffiti in Scotland too. In the late 1980s there was a story going around (I've heard many people insist since that it was true) that someone in Dundee had spray painted "FREE MANDELA" on the side of an Italian restaurant. The very next day a huge queue had formed outside the restaurant waiting for it to open, with locals eager to try out this new delicacy.

In their defence, there are some beautiful murals and art work on some buildings over here: it's not just plain vandalism (though whether this still constitutes vandalism is of course open to discussion ... just not here!). In actual fact, there is a culture of painting murals in many small towns and villages in Sardinia. Probably the most famous is Orgosolo, about 2 hours' drive from Cagliari near the city of Nuoro. In fact, Orgosolo is very close to Dorgali where I was conducting my bilingualism research (see Chapter 11), so I decided to take a visit one day. It is really spectacular to see. The art work is stunning. Like an open-air art gallery to be appreciated by all.

There is also a small town just a short drive north of Cagliari called San Sperate, which is home to a small community of artists (a kind of Sardinian Kirkcudbright, for those of you that know your Scottish geography). The internationally acclaimed sculptor Pinuccio Sciola was born in San Sperate and returned there after several years making a name for himself abroad. There is an open-air museum in the town that is dedicated to his work and is certainly worth a visit. In San Sperate, you will find a fine number of resplendent murals strewn all over the walls of public and private property all throughout the town. It is far from being an eyesore, and certainly far removed from the graffiti that I witness living in and around the city in Cagliari.

I think one of the differences between the UK and Italy, and something that does bother me most, is that here in Italy you see graffiti much more on private property as well as on public buildings. There doesn't seem to be the same level of respect extended to homeowners as perhaps there is in Scotland. I did begin to think that it might only be a problem in Cagliari but as I've travelled around Italy in the last few years I've noticed that it is not unique to Cagliari at all.

Stefania and I spent a weekend in Lucca a few years ago, in Tuscany. A beautiful, historical city encircled by an ancient wall. It's a picturesque little place where the majority of people go around the town centre in bikes. The architecture is breathtaking and it has a lovely atmosphere. However, even there I was struck by the graffiti in and around the centre. Indeed, we stood and watched a group of teenagers begin to spray paint a wall with some inane message right in front of us when we were there. I was about to intervene as no-one else seemed to be bothered, but luckily a local policeman had actually witnessed the whole thing and approached the youngsters.

What was even more astonishing (and disconcerting), however, was that the teenagers appeared to get away with it, receiving only as much as a telling off and to be told to get on their way. I didn't see any personal details being taken down or any handcuffs being produced. Well, perhaps I'm exaggerating now but come on ... some kind of chastisement was merited surely! (sorry did I give the impression earlier that my heart leans to the left? ... forget it! not when it comes to justifiably punishing some spotty and recalcitrant adolescents who have ruined some magnificent architecture). It was like a referee giving out a yellow card for witnessing a big, burly defender punching the lights out of the scrawny opposition striker as he was running in on goal.

The high level of tolerance and apparent lack of preoccupation demonstrated by the Italians towards their graffiti-splayed buildings contrasts with the way they are always carefully and immaculately turned out, and I don't mean for formal occasions such as weddings, baptisms, first communions and so on. I mean even if they're going for a stroll down the city centre to do some window shopping.

Fare la passeggiata literally means "taking a stroll" however there is an added significance to doing it in the evening, which basically means to walk up and down the main street, looking in shop windows and bumping into friends, and it is a key cultural activity over here.

I still remember the first time that I came over to visit Stefania, a matter of months after we first met. I had no clue about Italian culture then (I had no clue about a great many things it should be said). Indeed, I had never visited Italy before at this point in my life, so when she announced to me that we were going out for a *passeggiata*, and that I should get ready to go out, I immediately changed into a comfortable pair of trousers, a pair of trainers and my nice warm duffle coat (it was winter). Well, we were going out for a walk... it made perfect sense. She took one look at me before we left the house and said, "get changed". After I was instructed about what to put on, I felt as if we were going out for a wedding. I think she even had to ask her dad to borrow one of his 'smart' overcoats. Not something I owned at the time, being the cool and trendy student that I was. However, I would like to qualify this statement about the elegance of the Italians to point out that, despite their preoccupation with being smart while taking a stroll down the street, they tend to dress down somewhat when at home. It's not unusual for Italians of all ages, particularly the more elderly citizens to own a tracksuit (dare I say, shell-suit) that they change into as soon as they arrive home, or for other, similarly less formal, occasions. They even have a word for it: a *"canadese"*. A Canadian. I have no idea why they name it after the North American country, but there you go. It's an important part of the Italian's wardrobe. A bunch of neds if you ask me.

I've grown to like *la passeggiata*. It is a quintessentially Italian thing to do. And it's just so **not** a Scottish thing to do. We would just consider it a complete waste of our time. Bear in mind the timing here. *La passeggiata* is done in the evenings, around 7-8pm, when all the shops are still open, and the city centre is bustling. All year round. In Scotland at that time the city centre is usually deserted, especially in the winter months. Most people will be back home from work, wrapped up inside the house with the heating on and reluctant to go back out again. Indeed, if you do find yourself in need of something at that time of night, you would probably go to your nearest 24-hour supermarket and get in and out as fast as you can. You would probably do it with your head down, hoping not to bump into someone you know who would catch you buying the latest fashions to come out in the Georgina line[4].

Instead, in Italy, you wander up and down the city centre streets for an hour or so, and, more often than not, will bump into someone you will know. After a few months of us moving I could see that Cagliari is quite a small city after all, and that there are so many connections. For example, Stefania will say "oh you'll know him, he's the cousin of the barber's son, you know, who's older sister is married to that guy you play football with". What? Can you run that past me again? Honestly, it's like living in Kilmarnock.

Anyway, the other (main) reason I like *la passeggiata* is that it is usually accompanied by a stop at the pizzeria. I don't mean a sit-down pizzeria and stopping to buy a huge pizza. No, I'm

---

[4] Any resemblance to the fashion line of a well-known high street supermarket chain is purely coincidental. Indeed, for the record I must state that I have no problem whatsoever with the quality of the clothes that one can find in one's local Asda superstore. Indeed I can often be found sporting some of these fine and elegantly designed garments myself. Well, perhaps not that often. Let's just say "on occasion".

talking about buying a *pizzetta* (a little pizza) or a *pizza al taglio* (literally: a cut pizza). A *pizzetta* or a *pizza al taglio* is a rectangular slice of pizza that is doubled-over and eaten directly from the wrapping, and you continue your *passeggiata* while eating this culinary delight. I love them. You can get any flavour you like (well, within reason: don't advertise your status as a foreigner by ordering ham and pineapple ... I would never do such a thing. Honestly ham on a pizza? don't be daft). The most common flavours of *pizzetta* are *margherita* (obviously), *napoletana* (which is capers and anchovies: absolutely delicious!), *wurstel e cipolla* (frankfurter and onion) and *salsiccia* (dried sausage). You should only really eat one as it's close to dinner time, but I usually end up having two or three ... or even four. You know, just to try them. As the well-known expression goes over here ... who ate all the *pizzetta al taglios*?

In Cagliari, *la passeggiata* is done mostly in *via Garibaldi* and *via Manno*, right next to the historical city centre, and it's where, amongst other things, the highly desirable (and highly expensive) fashion boutique stores are found. Stefania told me once, and I do warn you that she is prone to exaggeration, that the shops that store the high end of the fashion market open firstly in Milan, then Rome, and then it's Cagliari. Apparently, there is a bit of money going around Cagliari. However, you wouldn't necessarily know it by looking at some parts of the city. Or maybe that's just the graffiti.

CHAPTER NINETEEN

Carnevale

It's virtually impossible to escape the fact that, in Italy when you get to February, it's carnival time – or simply *Carnevale*, as they like to call it here. *Carnevale* actually stretches from the day after the Epiphany (6th January) until Ash Wednesday, and the festivities culminate in celebrations on *Giovedì Grasso* (the Thursday before Ash Wednesday), *Martedì Grasso* (known all over the world as *Mardi gras* – the day before Ash Wednesday), and the weekend in-between.

I love it. It's just something that I never ever experienced as a child, and in some respects, I feel like I missed out. I suppose I'm just not used to celebrating at this time of the year, so it is a refreshing change to the dreary, dank days of January and February where one is trying to shake off some of those Post-Festive Season blues. The whole idea of *Carnevale* is quite simply not part of our culture in the UK (unless something has dramatically changed in the last few years). And that's a mistake in my book.

I still remember this slightly bizarre conversation that I had with Marcello, one of Stefania's friends, about the topic of *Carnevale* during one of my earlier visits to Sardinia. Marcello could speak reasonable English and would always insist that I would speak to him in English, even though I was just as keen to speak in Italian, as I was learning at the time. Anyway, in order to keep the peace, I would speak to him in English and the conversation went more or less like this:

Marcello: *"What do you do then in Scotland for Carnival time?"*

Me: *"Well, we don't really do anything"*

Marcello: *"What do you mean you don't do anything?"* [said in a rather aggressive, incredulous tone]

Me: *"Well, we do have Pancake Tuesday"*

Marcello: *"Oh, what's that then? Is that like our martedì grasso?"*

Me: *"Eh, kind of. Well, basically we all stay at home and make pancakes for dinner rather than what we would normally eat"*

Marcello: *"Oh that sounds nice* [but clearly thinking this sounds completely shite]. *And do you dress up?"*

Me: *"Nope"*

Marcello: *"Oh. And what else do you do?"*

Me: *"Well, that's about it really"*

Marcello: *"And when do you do this? Does it happen a lot between New Year and Ash Wednesday?"*

Me: *"Ash what? No, no. It only happens on Pancake Tuesday. Actually, if you're posh or a Joe Bloggs who's trying to pretend they're posh, you call it Shrove Tuesday. But most people just call it Pancake Tuesday"*

Marcello: *"Joe who? I don't think I know him. Is he a singer?"*

Me: *"Oh, just forget it"*

Actually, I think at this point I decided to *dress up* Pancake Tuesday (excuse the pun) and talked about it as if it were one of the highlights in the Scottish social calendar, where men dress up in skirts, and there's lots of music and dancing, and speeches and recitals of poems. As well as lots of whisky. There might even be fireworks at the end of the night. I was actually just describing a fairly typical Burns Supper, but I did it only because he was doing my nut in and I didn't want him to get away with thinking that we were completely shite when it came to celebrating *Carnevale*. I did it even though I knew fine well that I was being slightly parsimonious with the truth. Well, ok, I was lying.

Funnily enough we don't see Marcello much anymore. He's probably walking around somewhere in Cagliari telling anyone who's willing to listen to him (not many, I would hazard a guess) that Scotland is an amazing country that amongst all its other attributes, celebrates *Carnevale* in style.

Of course, instead of *Carnevale*, we have Halloween. That's our opportunity to dress up. The only (fairly large) difference is that Halloween usually lasts one day rather than one month. Indeed, Halloween is something that's actually starting to creep into the Italian culture now. The only thing is that they've taken on the very ghoulish and macabre side to Halloween. So, kids get dressed up as vampires, witches, ghosts and draculas, and many other kinds of gruesome characters.

This is another cultural difference, because, for me, Halloween is not (only) about the ghoulish side of things. It's about dressing up in whatever way you like – a bit like it is for *Carnevale*, really. So, for Halloween in Scotland you could dress up as a cartoon character, a Disney princess, a sailor, a pirate, or just about anything really.

I still have vivid memories of when I dressed up as a Rubik's cube one year (it was the 1980s after all). It was a home-made costume, as the vast majority were in those days, unlike the commercialised tat that people get dressed up in nowadays. Basically, it was a cardboard box with a hole cut in the middle so it could fit around my head, thus I was able to wear it around my torso. It was coloured in different paints to look like a multi-coloured Rubik's cube. It looked good and provoked (mostly positive) comment in every household we visited. Ingenious. I was happy as Larry. I thought I'd be the talk of the town for my imaginative and innovative costume. My best Halloween yet.

That was, until the rain came on. All the paint started dripping off and I started to look like a Rubik's cube having a bad mascara day. It was awful. One of the mums, whose home we visited, took pity on me and thought it'd be a great idea to cover me with a black bin-bag. That just made it worse. I was bare affronted. I just looked like a square-shaped walking bin bag, rather than an ingeniously creative Rubik's cube. I was the talk of the town right enough. Just not for the reasons I wanted. I was the never the same since. That Halloween changed me forever.

In Italy, for *Carnevale*, the kids (and most of the adults, it should be added) get dressed up in costumes of all kinds of various vibrant and gaudy colours: from clowns and princesses and Disney characters to ballerinas, witches and nuns, and everything else in-between (and that's just the men). It's bright, it's colourful and it's fun. There's music, dancing and lots and lots of food.

One of the main accompaniments to this period of *Carnevale* are the sweets that are produced. *Zeppole* or *Frittelle* are the main ones, which to me are exactly the same apart from the shape, and are spookily similar to our doughnuts. The *pasticceria* and the bars announce in their shop windows that there will be fresh *zeppole stasera* (this evening), as a way to entice you in. These homemade signs are everywhere in this period. I still remember the excitement on my first visit to Sardinia, where just after the Epiphany (6th January), the bars began to put these signs in their windows and the level of expectation and excitement was palpable. They take their sweets seriously over here. For me, however, the best *zeppole* are the ones made at home, as they will often have an extra wee kick in them: a hint (sometimes more than a hint) of *grappa* or *acquavite* (which is a Sardinian kind of liqueur/firewater) which gives it some extra flavour. Stefania is particularly adept at making these acquavite-based *zeppole* (amongst several other things I should add).

The other sweets made in this period are *Chiacchiere* (chit-chats), or sometimes referred to as *Bugie* (lies), depending on which part of Italy you're from. I like how they're called (innocent) 'chit-chats' in one area of Italy, but 'lies' in another. Anyway, they're quite simple really, but surprisingly delicious. They're made of a simple, short-crust kind of pastry, baked in the oven and then covered in icing sugar. Much less heavy than the *zeppole*, but no less tasty.

I lose count of the number of parties and festivities going on during *Carnevale*. The kids get dressed up several times in the few weeks around Carnevale but especially around *giovedì grasso* and *martedì grasso*. It seems that everywhere we're going, we have to get them dressed up.

Me: *"Come on, you need to get to the doctors, you're not feeling well"*

Finn: *"Wait a minute, dad. I'll need to put my Olaf costume on"*

Well, it's not quite that bad, but it's not far off it. One year they had a *Carnevale* party at the school, one at the Church, one at the Basketball team (where Luca and Anna were playing for the local team), one at the Scouts, another one because it was the birthday party of one of the friends of the kids (who wanted to have her party as a *Carnevale* party), and that's fairly typical.

On the Sunday between *giovedì grasso* and *martedì grasso*, we sometimes take part in the *Carnevale* procession that takes place in the historical centre of Cagliari - another opportunity to get dressed up. There are just as many adults dressed up there as kids. There is a marching band, people driving *Ape* (see Chapter 9), which are used as motorised floats, with lots of different human-sized papier-mâché figures placed on top, and lots of singing and chanting. It is chaos.

Apparently, the best Carnival parade to go to in Sardinia is in Oristano, called *Sa Sartiglia*, where amongst all the usual stuff, they have a medieval style competition where knights on horseback have to insert their sword into a tiny, star-shaped ring, that hangs dangling from a rope, while going at full speed. They also do acrobatic stunts on horseback and, aside from the spectacle, it is clearly quite dangerous and there have been reports of some serious injuries, and even fatalities, over the years.

Another side to *Carnevale* are the *coriandoli*, which are basically confetti for kids and the *stelle filanti* (multi-coloured streamers made from paper). They get thrown everywhere: inside, outside, in houses, in schools, in the streets, in the car. Yes, everywhere. The *coriandoli* are the worst. Thousands and thousands of tiny wee bits of coloured paper that seem to infiltrate your clothing somehow. You get home at night and while undressing you find your bedroom is seemingly converted into a temporary art studio. You find these wee bits of paper months afterwards, kicking about the cupboards and in other wee nooks and crannies.

Anyway, I digress somewhat. The point I'm making is that, for me, Halloween in Scotland is about dressing up in whichever way you want, much like *Carnevale* is over here. The only thing is that Halloween is creeping into the culture in Italy, but I don't see any evidence that *Carnevale* is creeping into the culture in Scotland. However, as I said earlier, Halloween in Italy is very much about the more ghoulish side of things rather than dressing up in any way you like. It took me a couple of years to work this out.

A year or two after we moved, I was asked to dress Finn up in a costume for the Halloween party at his nursery. He was only 18 months at the time, but all the children in the nursery were apparently coming dressed up, so I had to make an effort. We still had a Super Mario costume, left over from one of Luca's Halloweens back in Scotland. Perfect, I thought.

Mistake! When I took the wee man to his nursery that day to drop him off, the room was filled with ghosts, vampires, ghouls, witches and so on. And there was this wee Super Mario in the middle of it all with his red beret and blue dungarees, looking a picture. Fantastic. The nursery teachers looked at me completely bewildered when I dropped him off. They didn't question it, but I could tell there was something amiss. It was fairly obvious to the naked eye. But then, when you're Scottish living in Italy, you can get away with a lot of things by just quoting, "cultural difference". It certainly was a cultural difference on that occasion. I just hope Finn doesn't have the same nightmares about this experience as I had about being a walking bin-bag.

CHAPTER TWENTY

Papà, pappa e il papa

I would consider myself to be fluent in Italian now. Perhaps not a great achievement given we've been living over here for a while now, but nevertheless, I do take some level of satisfaction in understanding others and making myself understood. Still, despite my decent command of the language, I do still encounter situations where I can't understand exactly what is being said to me. This might be because of the use of idiom, or the use of words that sound the same to me but mean something entirely different, or also because of the residual use of some words from the Sardinian language that I have virtually no knowledge of.

I am slowly learning some of the idioms used

here in everyday language. An example would be *"mettersi nei panni degli altri"*, which means "putting yourself in someone else's shoes", although the Italian version literally translates as 'putting yourself in someone else's *clothes*', which might be considered rather more intrusive than merely putting on a stranger's pair of shoes.

Another one I like is *"portare un bambino a cavalluccio"*, which has the same meaning as our expression "giving a child a piggy back", only the Italians use the word "horseback" rather than "piggy back", which makes far more sense when you think about it. Why do we use an expression that means riding on a pig rather than a horse? Who knows? (The answer, in case you're interested, is that it has nothing to do with pigs, but was a mispronunciation of the Mediaeval word 'pick back' or 'pick pack', meaning to carry a pack on one's back).

The use of idioms - or not, as the case may be - does lead to some slight misunderstandings. A couple of years ago the mum of one of Anna's best friends, Renata, was explaining to me about the odd street layout in an area of Monserrato, the suburb of Cagliari where we live. Basically, I had noticed that the top half of one of the streets near where we live is indicated as being part of Monserrato, and the other half is indicated as being part of Selargius, the neighbouring 'town'. All on the same street. I was always intrigued by this.

I asked Renata, who seemed to know everything

about the local area, what it was all about. "*Qualcuno ha perso giocando a carte*", she replied. This translates as "Someone lost playing a game of cards". I was sure that this expression was idiom, intended to offer some kind of explanation, but I had no idea what, as I hadn't heard such an expression before. So I had to ask her for further clarification. "*No*", she insisted, "*I meant what I said, someone from the Council of Monserrato played a game of cards against someone from the Council of Selargius for that piece of land around 50 years ago and lost, and that's why the street is divided in two*". I just sat there, dumbfounded, looking at her like a goldfish. "*Ah, ok then*", I finally managed to volunteer, "*that explains it then*".

Another thing I have had some problems with is the correct pronunciation of certain words that sound very similar. An example is papà (pa - pa), pappa (pap- pa) and papa (pap - a). Depending on how it's pronounced this can mean "dad", "children's food" or "the Pope", respectively. So imagine my confusion when someone was telling me that their dad is the Pope, or when I would overhear a young mum asking her toddler to start eating her dad. It's all to do with the intonation: something that Italian mother-tongue speakers say is completely clear and unambiguous to the ear, while to non-mother-tongue Italian speakers like myself, it is less obvious.

Thus, I often get into these nonsensical arguments with Stefania where she tries to correct my pronunciation of a word. She basically repeats exactly what I've just said back to me. I then retort, "yes, I know. I said [insert word here]", and she repeats, "no you said [word] but you should say [word]", where the two words she's just spoken sound *exactly* the same. This argument usually goes on for several minutes in an ever-decreasing circle.

Apart from having to learn the subtleties of pronunciation, the non-mother-tongue Italian speaker has to learn other aspects about the language and culture over here. I've been told by my dear mother that I now talk with my hands, something I never ever used to do. I must do it just to fit in, but without realising. It is not an urban myth: everyone waves their hands about here when they talk. The other day I was driving past and I saw a man standing outside his car, talking quite vehemently on his mobile phone. Now remember he was on the phone. No one else, as far as he could know, was watching him. However, you would have thought he was conducting an orchestra. I wondered to myself: for whose benefit is he remonstrating with his hands? It must just be habit.

Another thing they do over here, which I find quite irritating, is to repeat "*ciao*" several times when they're saying goodbye. This effect is most dramatic when you're on the telephone. Once is not enough. At least three or four, even five, times is the norm. So you basically have to say "*ciao ciao ciao ciao*" in a way that they all run together one into the other like you're doing an impression of a steam train. Disturbingly I've begun to pick up on this habit, probably out of politeness so that people don't think I'm short-changing them by only saying goodbye once.

A hugely significant aspect regarding the language for people like me who are not mother-tongue speakers, although this is also an issue for mother-tongue speakers, is: when do you use the informal "tu" conjugation of the verbs, and when do you use the formal "Lei" version. This is not unique to Italian, of course, but it gets me tied up in knots almost on a daily basis. The basic guide is that you can use "tu" when you know the person well, or if they are younger than you: how much younger than you is not specified, however. If they're only a year or two younger than you, then probably best to use the "Lei". Of course, this can sometimes involve a very haphazard guess at people's ages, which can go horribly wrong.

To make matters even more confusing for foreigners like me, the formal "Lei" conjugation when you are addressing someone you don't know is **not** the 2nd person plural ("Voi") as it is in French (and many other languages), but is the 3rd person singular of "she", which you can imagine results in fairly confusing and bewildering conversations when you're at the beginning stage of learning Italian.

For example, someone may ask "*Cosa vorebbe Lei da bere?*", which would literally translate as "What would SHE like to drink?", but pragmatically translates as "*What would YOU like to drink?*", using the formal version. So I end up turning to look for Stefania and shouting across the room, "*What would you like to drink, Stefania?*", when instead the question was being addressed to me. This kind of scenario happened on several occasions to me after we first moved, but I think I'm now getting the hang of it. I'm now quite adept at spotting when questions are being addressed to me rather than when they're being addressed to a mysterious "she". It only took me about two years.

Another episode that illustrated this bizarre use of the 'double-meaning' of "she" to mean the formal "you" occurred with me in a school playground full of parents. Before I begin to recall the events of that day I should add that Italians (maybe I'm generalising, maybe it's only Sardinians) have this habit of shouting at you when they are recounting a story in which they are angry at someone else. Do you know what I mean? So, for example, if they have had a tortuous time at the post office that morning and were exasperated by the attitude of the post office clerk, they would recite the story to you as if YOU were the post office clerk and let off steam to you, as if YOU were to blame. I don't know why they do this, but they just do.

Anyway, to go back to my story. As I was waiting to pick up Anna from school, the grandfather of Anna's best friend (whom I knew quite well) arrived clearly very stressed and enraged and came straight towards me to stand beside me while waiting for the kids to exit the school. He didn't waste any time to embark on a furious and indignant rant about his daughter calling him up at the last minute to pick up his granddaughter. But the problem is that he was shouting at me, using the "she" conjugation of the verbs to refer to his daughter (but which could also be interpreted as the formal "you"). Thus, the other parents could hear him shouting in my face saying, *"I can't believe you've done this again. You call me up at the last minute to pick your daughter up from school. Can you not just organise yourself better and do it yourself? I mean what's your problem?"* and so on, whereas in actual fact, he was saying, *"I can't believe she's done this again. She calls me up at the last minute to pick her daughter up from school. Can she not just organise herself better and do it herself? I mean, what's her problem?"*. So, do you see why this 'double-usage' can become rather confusing?

Each Saturday morning I go to the *"Coldiretti"* (the farmer's market) in Monserrato. The fresh, local (0km, of course) produce is wonderful and I just love the atmosphere. They sell everything from fresh fruit and veg, eggs, honey, meat and cheese. You can get most of your weekly shopping here. I've struck up a rapport with the lady who sells fresh cheese: Maria's fresh ricotta is the most wonderful, creamy ricotta you could ever imagine. I can't buy it from anywhere else now – as one client put it, compared to Maria's ricotta you can actually taste the polystyrene if you buy the prepacked one in the supermarket. Anyway, after several months of exchanging a few words of conversation using the "*Lei*", I noticed that Maria suddenly changed to addressing me using the "*tu*". She is around my age, but probably 5 years or so older. I was in a moral quandary. What do I do? Should I reply using the "*tu*", or should she expect me to continue to address her using the "*Lei*" as she is a little older than me? For weeks I avoided the issue by exchanging our few words each Saturday in a way that meant I didn't have to address her directly (for example, you can say, "*come va?*" – how's it going?, instead of the usual "*come stai?*" – how are you?), but it got to the point where I was tired of no longer being natural in my communication with her. I decided to seek some advice from Stefania on the matter, sharing with her my angst at this most difficult and anxiety-provoking social dilemma. She just kind of shrugged her shoulders, "*What? What are you on about? Just use the "tu" and stop going on about it. For goodness sake*". Problem solved. I think I worry about this way more than I should.

It's still strange though, especially to a foreigner like me who has never had to confront this constant and delicate decision-making when talking to people in order to avoid making social gaffes. Our extended family now find ourselves in a bizarre situation at the dinner table where Flavio will address his in-laws using the formal *"Lei"* (probably rightly, giving them the respect of the formal address as their son-in-law), whereas I address the same people, with whom I have the same relationship, using the informal *"tu"*.

The reason for this dates back to my first visit coming over to meet the family, when I didn't speak Italian so well and so it was agreed (after some very careful negotiation work from Stefania) that it would be ok if I were to address them using the informal conjugation *"tu"*, as it was much easier and less confusing for me. After we were married, it seemed a little daft to resort back to the *"Lei"* as by then my Italian was better, so the informal address stuck.

It is quite normal to have a situation where you can know people quite intimately but have to use the formal *"Lei"* when speaking to them (my colleagues when I was working at Cagliari University, for example), but with people you've met for the first time, even to a shop assistant, for example, to use the informal *"tu"*. To make matters even more complicated, it is even possible to use the *"Lei"* in certain contexts and the *"tu"* in others WITH THE SAME PERSON. For example, I was told by a teacher that I know that she would use the *"Lei"* to parents (and vice-versa) while in the school, say for a parents' evening, but then out of the school, perhaps when meeting up a party where they might have shared friends, she would revert to using the *"tu"*. I find this just bizarre. I told Stefania about this and she simply said, "*that's nonsense. I've never heard of anything like that*". She should know. She invented the Italian language.

After we had been living in our apartment for several months, it seemed appropriate for Stefania to suggest to Signor and Signora Rossi that we could use the "*tu*" rather than the "*Lei*", and address each other with our first names. Signora Rossi agreed immediately, however, Stefania noticed that there was some reluctance on Signor Rossi's part to do the same. He appeared to be a little uncomfortable at the idea. Not because he didn't like us. Quite the contrary. He was always so friendly and one might say "informal" in all other aspects of his behaviour towards us. But, as he explained another time, months afterwards, he didn't even use the "*tu*" when addressing his parents! We felt honoured that he did agree to use the "*tu*" with us, despite his initial reluctance.

Yet another exasperating thing people do over here is to say "*è niente*" (it's nothing) just before they embark on saying something quite important. I thought this was an exclusively Sardinian habit but a couple of weeks ago I was listening to one of the national radio programmes, where listeners call in to recount some hilarious episode that has recently happened to befall them. Incidentally, just in case you happen to find yourself switching on a radio in Italy, the Radio Due programme is called "*il ruggito del coniglio*" - the roar of the rabbit - and is one of the most significant and successful radio programmes in the whole of Italy. Anyway, this guy called in and began his story, "*è niente, allora è successo che* ...." (it's nothing. well, what happened was ...).

I don't know why, but I lost it. I started shouting at the radio, "FOR FUCK'S SAKE. IF IT'S NOTHING, WHY THE FUCK DID YOU TAKE THE TROUBLE TO PHONE IN TO THIS RADIO SHOW, YOU IGNORANT BASTARD? AND IF IT'S NOTHING, WHY DO YOU HAVE TO SUBJECT US TO YOUR INSIGNIFICANT, SHITEY STORY?" Luckily, I was alone in the car at the time. Actually, now that I think about it, it was probably just stress as I was approaching a roundabout when it happened.

To be fair to the Italians, they do have some lovely words that are very economical in their use, whereby, for the same meaning to be transmitted in English, you would have to use several words. A good example of this is "*figurati!*". This is usually used as a response after someone thanks you for doing something for them. It would probably be translated literally as "go and figure", which sounds horribly American, and also doesn't convey the true meaning underlying the expression. What it really means is "Don't worry about it. It was actually a pleasure and I'm happy that I was able to be of some help". Twenty-one words in English for the price of one in Italian. Not bad, eh?

One thing you do notice after living over here for many years is the proliferation of English words in the Italian language. There are many English words in the Italian vocabulary. Here are just a few that I hear all the time over here: okay, shopping, computer, privacy, charm, break (to mean a pause from work), business, hotel, poster, snack, ticket, weekend, pizza, panini, antipasto, spaghetti, pesto, lasagne, cappuccino, pasta. Oh, wait a minute. Those last ones are actually Italian words that we use in English. Maybe I should just keep quiet.

The thing is, however, they seem to be very insensitive to the use of English swear words. You can see English swear words written all over the place, especially on clothes for some reason. One of our dear friends, Laura, owns a t-shirt with the following slogan written in large lettering: DON'T TOUCH MY FUCKING BAG. She insists it was a gift and never, ever goes out of the house with it on, but I have been given the honour of being shown the horribly distasteful garment. Maybe I'm just old-fashioned, but come on. That's just taking things too far.

Stefania recalls the dance routine she did when she was a teenager, that was loosely based on the music of Michael Jackson's album Bad. They were all dressed as kids "from the streets" with "FUCK YOU" and various other offensive slogans written all over their shorts and t-shirts. When she thinks about it now she can't believe how they got away with it, but then, when it's not your mother-tongue, it probably doesn't seem as distasteful or objectionable. Well, that's her excuse. Frankly, I was just shocked and dismayed. Actually, I was fucking outraged.

CHAPTER TWENTY-ONE

Baci

In addition to grappling with the language, a foreigner living in Italy has to learn some basic customs that make up your everyday life. For example, giving kisses (*baci*) is an everyday occurrence over here when you meet or bump into someone you know. Of course, you don't kiss everyone you happen to know (well, you could if you wanted but you might find people will start to cross the street to avoid you), so there's a lot to consider about who, and in what circumstances, do you kiss someone.

The first thing to consider is how well you know the person. But then that doesn't mean that you always kiss all the people with whom you use the informal *"tu"* conjugation of the verbs, and never kiss any of the people with whom you use the formal *"Lei"* conjugation. It is quite feasible to kiss people with whom you address using the *"Lei"*, and **not** kiss people with whom you address using the *"tu"*. The two things are unrelated. You see why I get confused over here?

They do kiss much more often here than we do in Scotland. One day I saw a guy get out of his car at traffic lights (thankfully they were red at the time), in order to exchange *baci* with a car full of clearly intimate friends. I just watched him, flabbergasted, as the lights eventually turned to green and the horns started to sound. He just nonchalantly returned to his car, not appearing to give two hoots (sorry, I couldn't resist) about the inconvenience imposed on the traffic behind him. In fact, as the horns got louder he even gesticulated with his arm in a rather unpleasant way and shouted out some offensive remark to the horn-blowers. As if to say, "what's your problem? The *baci* are more important here".

At least in Italy, what is straight-forward is that this more intimate greeting is always the same - a kiss on each cheek. That's the same whether it's a man kissing a woman, a woman kissing a woman, or a man kissing a man. Yes, that's right. A man kissing a man. I must stress that I have no problem whatsoever with this. I am neither homophobic nor a closet homosexual, and while it is not something that is part of the Scottish culture (far from it, as I will describe below), I just accept it as part of the culture where I now live my life. Kissing men is part of my daily routine in a way that I just never would have considered for a nano-second if you had told me 20 years ago.

As I say, I have no problem with it. Whether I could say the same for many of my good friends back in Scotland, is another matter. I've always considered the fixation on homosexuality as a weirdly West of Scotland anachronism, that in my experience anyway, still shows little sign of abating. For example, if you decide to order a cocacola in the pub, or any other soft drink, or indeed, even a glass of wine in Scotland, you are immediately designated as being homosexual, or to use the West of Scotland vernacular, a poof[5].

I still remember vividly the reaction I got one Saturday night in August many years ago (as much as 20 years ago now), when I announced to my friends in the pub that Stefania and I had just come straight from attending the Bolshoi Ballet Company's interpretation of Midsummer Night's Dream at a theatre in Edinburgh. The response this news received, perhaps rather unsurprisingly to

---

[5] I apologise profusely to anyone who might be offended by this last remark. It is in no way intended to offend but instead to highlight the crass and, quite frankly, ignorant attitude that still prevails in the West of Scotland towards people who are gay, and where, for some reason, the sexual orientation of gay people (usually men) is used as a means to poke fun at others. I wholeheartedly disagree with such a practice. I believe (and hope) it is not as diffuse as it once was.

many of you, was to immediately discuss my sexuality. I remember thinking at the time how odd it was to be ascribed as homosexual after going to see a theatrical performance with one's girlfriend. But there you go.

There doesn't seem to be the same association made over here. You can freely go to the theatre, the ballet, the opera, even a museum and not have your sexuality even barely mentioned. It's quite liberating, actually.

Another thing that they say over here and I can NEVER imagine happening back in Scotland is that male friends quite often greet each other with the hail "*Ciao bello*" ("Hi gorgeous" or "Hi beautiful"), and I can assure you it is not said in a sarcastic or ironic manner. It's meant as a warm, affectionate way to say hello to someone you like. Believe it or not, I've had it said to me hundreds of times over here.

I've been called many, many things by my dear friends in Scotland, but I can reveal that I have never, ever been addressed to as "gorgeous", "handsome" or "beautiful" by them back home, in all the years I lived there. Now, I know that for those of you that have seen me in the flesh, there may be an obvious reason for this, but I think it goes beyond mere aesthetics. It just wouldn't feel comfortable to address your male friend in Scotland as being "beautiful" because the repercussions would be far too great - aside from the 'fear' (ridiculous, I know) that some may have of being thought of as gay, it would not be met with any great enthusiasm from the receiver anyway. Actually, the 'receiver' of the compliment may never look at you the same way again. You might as well consider your friendship with the receiver as terminated henceforth, never to be seen with each other again.

Not so long ago I was outside doing my daily chore (amongst many others, of course) of putting the rubbish out. One of the neighbours with whom I have a fairly convivial relationship was also doing the same thing. His name is Omero (Homer in English). We chat every so often and get on well. He's from Northern Italy and we often joke that we are the northern Europeans trying to cope with the dry, hot and arid Mediterranean climate, while reminiscing of the times when we would spend our days happily underneath an umbrella or locked away in our houses waiting for the rain to pass. Omero is a neighbour. I don't know him that well, but we do get on ok and often chat away easily.

Anyway, he saw me approaching the bins and shouted out "*Ciao bello!*" and I noticed who it was and replied, "*Ciao Amore*", instead of "*Ciao Omero*". I was tired and I did intend to say "*Ciao Omero*" but it just came out all wrong. For those not up to speed with their Italian, "*Ciao Amore*" would translate as "*Hi darling*". So basically, you had the following exchange of words, "*Hi Gorgeous*". Response: "*Hi darling*". What astounded me further was that Omero hardly batted an eyelid. He just laughed and then continued on with the conversation as if nothing had happened. If it had happened in Scotland, there would probably be a steward's inquiry and the friendship would immediately be under threat.

Last summer I finally relented to the peer pressure of all the middle-aged males around me and bought a small manbag, the kind that can store your wallet, phone and keys. You hang it over your shoulder in a way that is not that dissimilar to how a woman might use their handbag. It's actually very practical. Especially during the summer (and even during spring and autumn), where it's so warm so you don't have a coat or jacket when going out. So where else can you keep these essential items? Ergo, the use of my manbag.

Of course, need I add, my manbag stays in Sardinia. On my visits back to Scotland I have not even thought twice about bringing it with me. Not only because the climate dictates that I would probably not need it, but I would NEVER be seen going around with one of these essential accessories in Scotland. The piss-taking would be absolutely relentless. I can just imagine it, as I would walk into the pub, "*Hey Fraser, whaur's yer high heels and yer make-up to go with your handbag, ya big jessie*". Sad, yet true.

Don't misunderstand me here. I'm not saying that attitudes towards homosexuality are more modern and liberal over here. Quite the contrary actually. I think Scotland is generally quite forward-thinking when it comes to attitudes towards homosexuality, which was demonstrated clearly during the opening ceremony of the Commonwealth Games in 2014 in Glasgow, where we made a big show of the fact that we were an open and liberal country when it comes to civil partnerships and same-sex relationships. The situation is rather different over here, and one may argue that this is especially true because of the influence of the Catholic church.

I still remember overhearing a conversation in the little grocery shop near our house between two middle-aged women. They were well-dressed and well-educated - in fact, I managed to pick up from the conversation that one was a teacher. They were talking about a young lad that they both knew, and they were saying how disgraceful it was that he had declared his homosexuality - an embarrassment to his family and how awful it must be for his parents. I couldn't believe my ears. I felt like H.G. Wells had kidnapped me and I had woken up in the 1920s. However, as I've said in another chapter, the values and mores are generally rather traditional and stuck in the past over here (see chapter 16). Sometimes this may be considered a positive thing, but on other occasions not so.

I suppose what I'm trying to say is that homosexuality is not used in a derogatory way in Italy, as it might be in Scotland. For example, to put others down just because you happen to go to a performance of ballet at the theatre, or you want to order a ginger ale and blackcurrant on a night out. Which, despite the more negative attitudes towards homosexuality generally in Italy, is something at least. Well, the point is, I can use my manbag in peace.

CHAPTER TWENTY-TWO

Montalbano sono

Moving to a new country means that you are exposed to all aspects of the culture, and that includes television. When I say to friends and family back in Scotland that there is a lot of Italian television that I like, they usually look at me as if I'm daft. For some reason, a lot of people abroad have the idea that Italian television is full of scantily-clad girls prancing about on the set of various game shows and tv quizzes. The truth is that, unfortunately, that does exist too, but these programmes are usually on Silvio Berlusconi's channels - Canale 5 and Italia 1 - which we don't watch, I'm happy to point out. How Berlusconi, a former Prime Minister, and key political figure in Italy for over 25 years can own two of the country's main television channels is not a topic that will be discussed in this book. Let's just accept it as ridiculous and move on.

In addition to all the nonsense shown on Canale 5 and Italia 1, there is actually a lot of high quality television: documentaries, political discussion, and various other decent entertainment shows, and most of these are on the national broadcaster channels - Rai Uno, Rai Due and Rai Tre (the equivalent of the BBC), and also on an independent channel called La 7.

My favourite television programme over here - indeed, I'm willing to stick my neck out here and say my favourite television series ever - is *Il Commisario Montalbano* (Inspector Montalbano). I was first introduced to the wonders of Montalbano back in 2000 when it was first broadcast on Rai Uno, while we were over visiting Sardinia on holiday. I fell in love with it immediately. We even had a satellite dish installed in our house in Edinburgh so that we could follow the trials and tribulations of *Montalbano* from a distance.

I've always loved crime programmes, even as far back as when I was a child, from the days of The Sweeney, and the Professionals, all the way through to Morse, Frost and Rebus, to name just a few. But *Montalbano* is different. In my opinion, anyway.

Firstly, it's set in Sicily and the backdrop is phenomenally beautiful. The small coastal village where *Montalbano* lives, and where he regularly eats his seafood delicacies at the local *trattoria*, just looks scrumptious[6]. As does his apartment, which sits right on the sea front, and from where he goes into the sea each morning for his early morning dip. The story lines are superb - based on the novels by the wonderfully talented Andrea Camilleri (still going strong to this day as he approaches his 93rd birthday).

The acting is second to none, not only by the main actor, Luca Zingaretti, who plays Montalbano, but there are also wonderful cameo roles played by local people and fantastic characterisations of many of the supporting actors (Mimi, Cattarella, and Fazio for those *Montalbano* fanatics amongst you). Luca Zingaretti is considered one of the finest actors that Italy has produced (we had the pleasure of seeing that for ourselves when he came to Cagliari to perform a one-man play a few years ago), and he has become quite a celebrity in Italy, mostly because of his portrayal of Montalbano. Lastly, but not leastly, there is the beautiful, yet haunting soundtrack. Need I say more? I doubt it. I know that in recent years *Il Commissario Montalbano* has begun to be

---

[6] Incidentally, if you find yourself in Cagliari and want to eat in a 'Montalbano' restaurant then I highly recommend you go to Lo Zenit or Non Solo Mare, in Giorgino, the fisherman's village just a few km from Cagliari. Book ahead though. They are the most popular restaurants in the area and you'll soon discover why. They are situated right on the beach looking out to sea.

shown in the UK, on BBC 4, and it has received a warm and enthusiastic response from those who watch it. I believe it's quickly gaining a cult status in the UK.

Every couple of years or so, a new series of *Il Commissario Montalbano* is produced and usually shown on Monday nights on Rai Uno. The build-up goes on for weeks. There are adverts on tv, on radio and even adverts on billboards, announcing the return of Italy's favourite detective. The excitement is undeniable. Thankfully each new series always lives up to the high expectations placed upon it. I wouldn't want to think of the consequences if it didn't. It could trigger a premature general election (not entirely unlikely for over here, I should add).

One of Montalbano's catchphrases occurs when he answers the telephone and says simply in his gruff voice, "*Montalbano sono*" (meaning "*It's Montalbano*" but literally translates as "I'm Montalbano"). This always reminds me of a story that happened many years ago, when I was a student in England. I shared a flat with two Irish lads and Adriano, an Italian student from near Venice, who was introduced to me by Stefania. We all got on really well and it was a great flat. We had a lot of laughs.

Adriano spoke English quite well but he was still learning some aspects. One of the things he used to do was reply to the telephone with "*Hello, I'm Adriano*". The Irish lads used to giggle away as if it was the funniest thing they'd ever heard in their lives. Of course, I was learning Italian at this time, and knew exactly why he would respond in this way, and so I would take the highbrow intellectual line - while stifling my own chuckles - and told them to stop sniggering at our Italian friend who was still learning some of the pragmatic aspects of the English language.

However, one day it was a step too far for the Irish boys when he left a written note for us sellotaped to the inside of the door, which he had written to inform us that he was going back home for the Christmas break and so wouldn't see us until January. He wanted to wish us all the best for the forthcoming festivities. "*Dear boys*", it began, "*I'm Adriano*". We didn't get beyond the first line. The Irish lads had just returned from being out all day on an end-of-term drinking session, and couldn't keep it in any more. They lost it. In amongst their roars of laughter, they would shout, "*Fraser, come on, help us out here. You're a psychologist. What the hell is wrong with this guy? Why does he feel the need to validate his own existence each day for some reason? Does he have multiple identities? Is he a spy? Or does he just have severe memory loss?*" This went on for about another half hour. Poor guy.

Another programme that is much loved over here is *Don Matteo*, also shown on *Rai Uno*, about a priest who independently investigates various crimes around the town, as well as attending to the ecclesiastical needs of the local parish. This fictional series, set in the beautiful Umbrian town of Gubbio, centres on the parish priest (*Don Matteo*, of course) who consistently outdoes and outthinks the local *Carabinieri* (for our purposes, the police, but I do try to explain the difference between the police and *Carabinieri* in a later chapter) and solves the surprisingly frequent incidence of murders and vicious assaults that occur in the surrounding area.

By the time I started watching *Don Matteo*, it was into its sixth series, and I have to confess, within a couple of episodes, I was hooked. It does have a rather formulaic storyline each time (though many a successful programme has relied on that in the past). However, the characterisation, and in particular, the relationship between the two main characters – *Don Matteo* and *Maresciallo* (Marshall) *Cecchini*, the policeman posted to Gubbio from Sicily, is very well done and entertaining. Each episode usually ends with a moral and religious message, sometimes even accompanied by an appropriate quote from the Bible, and repentance from the no-gooder, following the divine intervention of *Don Matteo*. Brilliant stuff!!!!

I laugh sometimes, imagining how this would go down in the UK on one of the main television channels – I just can't see Inspector Morse or Taggart suddenly quoting from the Bible as they catch their man, asking them to beg forgiveness from the Lord. *Don Matteo* is now in its 11th year and no-one has questioned how so many murders and horrific events could happen in such a small, beautiful and picturesque town in central Italy. But then, that's not the only unbelievable thing about the programme, so I think people are happy just to let that one go ...

Of course, I shouldn't be surprised that *Don Matteo* is so popular over here. As I've said in a previous chapter, religion still plays a pivotal role in everyday life in Italy. You can't live over here and escape the presence of religion, or Catholicism really, as you go about your daily business.

Most public buildings (schools, hospitals, town council buildings, and doctor's surgeries, to name a few) have the symbol of the crucifix attached to the wall. However, not long after we moved here, this ubiquitous aspect of Italian life was challenged by a mother of two children attending a school in northern Italy. She took her case to the European Court of Human Rights, citing that the use of the crucifix violated the secular principles that public schools in Italy are supposed to uphold. Initially she won her case, and the ruling had the consequence that ALL Italian schools should remove the crucifix from the classroom walls. The outcry from the general public, politicians, and of course, religious figures, in particular the Vatican, was unbelievable.

The main argument that seemed to be made, in amongst all this public outrage, was that the crucifix was not merely a religious symbol, but a cultural one, and one that was part of Italy's heritage and identity. And to take it away from all public buildings, and in particular its schools, was like cultural rape (excuse the hyperbole here, but this expression was actually used by someone when discussing the issue). Indeed, the Italian Government appealed the decision and won their appeal. In the end, it was ruled that there was no evidence that a crucifix hung in a classroom would influence pupils. It just served to remind me that, despite falling numbers who attend Church, and perhaps also falling numbers who consider themselves religious, it seems that Italy, for the time being at least, is still very much a Catholic country, and, in the main, seems to want to maintain this reputation.

It is not just public buildings where you find religious imagery. You find images in the unlikeliest of places. My local pharmacy, 100 yards from my house, has a silver-plated framed portrait of Jesus Christ, placed bizarrely on the top shelf, behind the counter, sitting amongst several boxes of pills and medicines. It is an odd juxtaposition. At first, I thought it was maybe for sale (though I had never seen any other similar religious artefacts for sale in the pharmacy). However, one day I discovered for sure that it was there for other reasons. I finally gathered up the courage and decided to test out my theory by asking the pharmacist how much the lovely framed picture of Jesus was. She just stared at me as if I had just alighted from my spaceship, and asked her to take me to her leader. She didn't even do me the courtesy of a response. Now there was an opportunity lost. For all she knew, I could have offered an inordinate amount of money for the image.

The influence of religion and the Church is also riddled throughout the Italian language. When children play hide-and-seek over here, the home base is known as "*la chiesa*", the church. So when kids run back to base without being caught by the 'seeker', you can hear them shout "*chiesa*" as they reach their destination. Another example is the use of a common expression over here, "*ogni morte di papa*" (for every death of the Pope) to indicate that you haven't seen someone, or done something, for a while. The increasing use of this idiom probably dates back to around the papacy of John Paul II whose tenure lasted from 1978 to 2005. Or maybe not. I'm speculating.

Sundays, while clearly not the same as they would have been around 20 years ago, are still clearly a day of rest, and usually spent with family having a huge meal that will go on for most of the day. In fact, a Sunday on a calendar over here is actually marked "*Festa*", which literally translates as "feast", but in modern parlance means "holiday". While it's true that this is changing rapidly (for example, the shopping centres scattered around the hinterlands of Cagliari and some of the city centre shops do now open on Sundays), you don't have to go that far out of Cagliari to the small towns and villages dotted around to get an idea of what it would have been like in Cagliari 20 years ago. In these smaller towns and villages, almost nothing at all is open on Sundays, and they are like ghost towns.

We often go to San Vito at weekends, about an hour's drive from Cagliari, where many of Stefania's relatives live, and where we have a house ourselves. We're well aware now that most of the shops are closed on Sunday, so we come prepared. It's a tranquil and peaceful setting, and we love it. And if the tranquillity gets too much, then we always have the option of switching on the telly. There's usually something good on.

CHAPTER TWENTY-THREE

Pasquetta

The Easter week starts with *Domenica delle Palme* (Palm Sunday), and ends with *Pasquetta* (Easter Monday), with lots of other stuff in-between. Easter is a major celebration over here, almost on the scale of Christmas and I just completely indulge myself in all the stuff that's going on. I really enjoy it.

On the morning of Palm Sunday you will see crowds flocking to the hundreds of palm sellers outside the churches. I say palm "sellers", but most of them will accept *"un'offerta"* (a donation) in exchange for a few leaves from a bit of tree. Actually, that's totally unfair. Some of the intricate designs that these people produce with the palm leaves are quite something: very artistic and aesthetically beautiful.

They range in size. They can be very small: for example, it's common over here to buy one and put it in your car, often slipped under the sun shield visor (there's usually a band you can slip it under), thus protecting you from any eventual car accidents. Of course, it works wonderfully well. There are no car accidents at all in Italy[7]. You can also buy slightly bigger ones to place in your house, and even bigger ones to put... actually I have no idea where the people who buy the large sized branches put them, after they've traipsed around town carrying a branch-sized bit of palm tree on Palm Sunday. Maybe in their garden? I've no idea.

The Sunday mass on Palm Sunday in our local church begins with the blessing of the palms outside in the open air, about 200 metres from the church in a small *piazza*. We then follow the priest to the church trying our very best not to appear as if we're racing ahead to grab a seat inside the church before everybody else. The church is always packed on Palm Sunday. And when I mean packed, I mean packed. Hundreds of people crammed in to

---

[7] This phrase represents the concept known in English as 'irony'. Of course it is not true that there are no car accidents in Italy, but nevertheless, I wish to emphasise that in no way, shape or form is the statement intended to offend those who believe that by sticking a bit of tree in their car they will be immune from any possible motor accidents on the roads.

the point that, if you suffered from claustrophobia, you would get out ... and quick! You can hardly move.

Mass is on almost every day from Palm Sunday onwards, culminating in the Easter Sunday ceremony. We usually spend the Easter weekend in San Vito, on the east coast of Sardinia, in the area where Stefania's father's family is from, and where Stefania's aunts, uncles and cousins still live. We're fortunate to have a house there that we use for these occasions, as well as during the summer time.

It's a beautiful area - known as *Sarrabus* in the south-eastern corner of the island - and has some of the most amazing beaches in the Mediterranean, as well as a peace and tranquillity that is just priceless. Thousands of *Cagliaritani* flock to this area in the summer time (and other parts of the year), just to get out of the city for a while and breath some nice, clean, fresh air.

The views of the night sky from our internal *cortile* (courtyard) in San Vito are breath-taking. Because of the lack of air pollution you can easily spot many of the constellations with the naked eye. And on the 10th August each year (the day of San Lorenzo in Italy), you get a stunning show of shooting stars constantly going off one after the other from about midnight onwards. One summer, a few years ago, friends of ours came over from Scotland to visit us in San Vito, and their stay with us coincided with San Lorenzo. We just lay out in the *cortile* looking up at the sky as one shooting star after another burst into life right above us, temporarily lighting up the night sky. It was spectacular.

Anyway, I digress. We usually spend our Easter weekend in San Vito. The first big meal is on the Saturday evening - the night before Easter Sunday - where all the family gets together for the usual long, drawn-out meal. Actually, this meal is a bit different as you are supposed to eat a little more frugally as you have to keep all the good things for the next day and the big Easter celebratory meal. However, despite this, the meal does still seem to take around 3 hours to complete. One of the delicacies you are supposed to eat during the Easter Saturday Evening meal is *la cordula*, which is basically the intestines of the animal. And it really does look like intestines. This is usually cooked on the fireplace using the spit, and it is surprisingly delicious. Of course, there is everything else that comes before this and after. The antipasti (cold meats, roasted vegetables, olives and so on), a plate or two of pasta, fruit, dessert and plenty of other stuff that I've already described in detail (see Buon lavoro!, chapter 11). This is what they mean by bring frugal.

At this point, there is the option of going to late evening mass, but we usually tend to defer this pleasure and wait until the following morning. No, really, I'm not being deliberately provocative or ironic here. It truly is a pleasure to go to mass in San Vito on Easter Sunday. It is quite an event.

First there is *l'incontro* (the meeting) in a little piazza near our house. This is where a large edify of Christ - carried on top of the shoulders of around six men on a plinth - meets a similarly-sized representation of the Madonna (Jesus' mum that is, not the American pop singer from the 1980s), that is being carried from the opposite direction. It's a very sombre affair, and when they meet, the veil of the Madonna effigy is raised to reveal her face, and there are flowers thrown from a balcony above on top of the two effigies in utter silence.

We then walk behind the two effigies to the local church, again trying hard not to be noticed walking too fast to try and get to the front in order to bag a seat inside. Once inside the church, the mass begins. The music is magnificent - there are beautiful harmonies from the choir, wonderful percussion, guitars, and other instruments that make up a stirring and emotional sound. It's also possible that the music in the church will be accompanied by the maestro Luigi Lai, who is arguably the finest player of the *launeddas* that has ever lived, and certainly the most famous, not just in Sardinia, but internationally. He is 82 years old now, and still going strong. We are privileged when he decides to play at his local church.

The *launeddas* is a very simple looking reed-based musical instrument, and indeed is not too dissimilar to the reeds that are used in bagpipes. The only major difference between the two is that while in Scotland a bag is used to generate the sound (or air stream), in the *launeddas* the player does the same thing using his cheeks, which swell up to the size of two small melons. It is remarkable to watch. And the sound that it produces is just magical. Enchanting and unique.

After mass, we all meet outside in the piazza in front of the church to exchange Easter wishes. As we have a house here and know quite a few people in the village, and also considering that many of Stefania's family live here, this can take a while. By the end I'm absolutely starving, and thus looking forward to my long, drawn-out meal.

I'm going to skip over the description of what we usually have to eat. We could be here all day. But needless to say, it is most enjoyable and very, very long. The rest of the day is usually spent visiting relatives, or going for a long walk in the country to try and burn some of the excesses indulged in over the previous four hours.

The following day is *Pasquetta* (Easter Monday: literally means 'little Easter'). I absolutely adore *Pasquetta*. Similar to the UK, *Pasquetta* is a national holiday and it is a good time to meet up with friends. The warm climate allows you to plan this well in advance, as you can be almost certain that the weather will be perfect.

The weather tends to be warm and sunny for Pasquetta (around 25oC), which is perfect for spending the entire day outdoors. *Pasquetta* often involves a trip into the countryside (*una scampagnata*) and (surprise, surprise) will often revolve around having an extravagant meal out in the open air, and more often than not, will involve cooking on a barbeque.

When I say 'barbeque', I don't mean a portable, three-legged barbeque that you can stick in the back of your car. As you'll have understood by now, they do things seriously over here when it comes to food. Many country parks come equipped with several huge, brick-built cooking pits. And it is not uncommon to see people cooking an entire *maialetto* (suckling pig) on the spit, as well as other whole pieces of animal. Not the usual burgers and sausages, that's for sure. There is no hiding place for the squeamish: whether you're vegetarian or not. If you decide to try some meat, it's undeniable that it has come from a dead animal.

The cooking pits are so popular that many of the busier parks now have a booking system: you book ahead and pay a nominal fee (e.g. €1 per adult and 50 cents per child) to have access to a decent-sized picnic bench and the cooking pit. Well worth the money. It means that, while it is busy, it is never too busy and you're not fighting over space. Indeed, in the park where we went one year (called *Sa Fogaia*, towards the middle of Sardinia, near a small town called Siddi), there was a lovely atmosphere: busy, but not too busy, and very friendly and sociable. The views of the surrounding hills and plateaus were splendid: because of the fine weather you could see for miles and miles around.

Just a short walk away from our picnic tables and cooking pit, there was an original *nuraghe*: an ancient, stone, conical-shaped tower that dates back to prehistoric times, where they were used as dwellings by one of the earliest recorded Mediterranean civilisations. There's so much I could write about the *nuraghe* - they are truly amazing and unique to Sardinia, but the truth is that they're actually quite difficult to describe. It's one of these things that you have to go and see for yourself. Many of these were built as far back as 2000BC. There is so little known about this *Nuragic* civilisation, yet they seemed to have led a fairly sophisticated existence, with facilities for cooking, hot water and comfortable dwellings, including a 'meeting room' where important decisions about the community were made.

The most famous *nuraghe* in Sardinia - and there are over 7000 of them in total - is in Barumini, about 45 miles north of Cagliari. I urge you to go and visit if you ever find yourself on the island. It's a unique experience that really takes you back in time, as you clamber in and around the *nuraghe's* internal structure. The *nuraghe* in Barumini is an UNESCO World Heritage Site and visitors - particularly those interested in archaeology and pre-historic life - come from all over the world to have a look. There is a museum and a visitor centre nearby and you can easily spend a whole day there. I had the pleasure (and honour) of working there for 3 months while helping the tourist guides perfect their English. So feel free to go and speak to them. They'll understand you perfectly well, even if they do speak with a slight Scottish accent. Anyway, back to the *Pasquetta*.

The only downside I would say about going on a *scampagnata*, or any outing in general, is the Italian habit of having to go in convoy to get there. Italians absolutely love their convoys. I'm sure I'm not the first person to comment on this peculiar Italian habit, but it's not until you actually live here that you realise how widespread and popular it is. It doesn't matter where you're going with a group of friends, the Italians like to do it in convoy. Even if it doesn't make any sense whatsoever to go to your destination in convoy (for example, you're going to a restaurant that is only 3 miles away from Cagliari and you all live in different parts of the city and would be taking different routes to get to the final destination), you still end up gathering at a pre-arranged meeting point and heading off from there.

Usually, during the convoys, you have to wait several times for several minutes during the journey for stragglers to catch up (e.g. they've been caught up at traffic lights or they've been stopped by the *Carabinieri*), and it becomes immensely frustrating. But, in Italy at least, it just seems that this is the way that things should be done, regardless of whether it's efficient or not.

For *Pasquetta* one year I had the audacity to suggest to a group of Stefania's friends that instead of congregating at the meeting point we could perhaps all make our own way to our final destination and meet there, rather than doing the journey all together and stopping every 2 kilometres. I got the usual looks, especially from Stefania. You know the look. I'm sure you've probably been on the receiving end too once or twice in your life. Probably more than once or twice if you have an Italian spouse. The 'look' conveys disgust and despair as to how you could possibly think of suggesting something so stupid (even though it is clearly more sensible) that would challenge everything that is dear to the Italian culture. And to do so in front of my friends too. What an embarrassment. So they decided to ignore my advice and we travelled in convoy. Again.

I shouldn't complain. Despite all the waiting for stragglers and stop-start nature of the journey, none of us had an accident on the way there, or on the way back. Those palm leaves really do work wonders.

CHAPTER TWENTY-FOUR

La strada nuova

Only 200 yards from our house lies the *Ponte di Emanuela Loi*. It's a fine bridge and a symbolic landmark for the surrounding area. It can be seen easily from all over Monserrato during the day, as it juts out into the sunlit sky, but also at night, as it is lit up spectacularly and can be seen from miles around. The bridge stretches across the 554 (or as the locals call it "*la cinque cinque quattro*"), which is one of the most important roads around Cagliari. The 554 takes you to all the suburbs of Cagliari and, arguably more ˙᠆ntly, to the south-east coastline, known as ᠌osso (the Red Border), from where ᠊ further east and north to *Villasimius*,

Costa Rei, and more frequently for us at least, to *San Vito* and the *Sarrabus* area of Sardinia.

The bridge was completed in 2009 and dedicated to Emanuela Loi, a local girl who was killed in Palermo by the Sicilian Mafia in 1992, while she was working in Sicily as a police officer. Emanuela was just 24 years old at the time of her murder. We moved to Sardinia just as the bridge was being completed and I've always been intrigued by the circumstances of Emanuela's demise. It didn't take me long to discover that Emanuela had been caught up in one of, if not the most, notorious and horrific episodes of Mafia criminal behaviour that Italy has ever witnessed. Indeed, it triggered for me the memories I had of reading about the episode in UK newspapers in the early 1990s, while I was a student at University.

What I didn't know then, but I do now, was that a Sardinian girl was one of victims of this most infamous and shocking set of events. So shocking it is known in Italy as "*La Strage di Via D'Amelio*", i.e. the Massacre of D'Amelio Street, where the assassinations took place. Let me give a bit of background.

Giovanni Falcone was a Sicilian Judge who for many years was building up a formidable reputation in Italy as someone who was strong and capable enough of taking on the might of the Mafia through several prosecutions. The highlight of his career was the process of having Cosa Nostra (the Italian name for the Sicilian Mafia for those who don't know) recognised as a criminal organisation in the legendary Maxi-trials that were held in Palermo in 1986-87.

On the day of May 23rd, 1992, Falcone flew from Rome to Palermo airport with his wife, but while he was being given his usual Police escort back to his home in the city, his car was blown to smithereens by a carefully planned and calculated assassination by the most senior members of the Sicilian mafia. The Mafia had identified Falcone (probably correctly) as the most serious and immediate threat that they had ever had to their way of living and to their freedom of "managing" the island.

It was the assassination of Falcone and his wife that I recall reading about in the press in the UK. It was a massive event at the time. It was widely considered that the Mafia had taken a step too far in their fight to control and "govern" Sicily, and the public outcry in Italy was unprecedented. What I hadn't realised was that 57 days afterwards, the Mafia murdered Judge Falcone's lifelong friend and colleague, Paolo Borsellino, in a car bomb just outside his mother's home in Palermo.

It was in this bomb that Emanuela and her four colleagues from the Police were caught up in, as they were posted there to protect Borsellino from any attempt on his life. Borsellino was fully aware that he would be targeted, as he and Falcone had worked so closely together on the various Mafia trials. He knew he was on borrowed time, but perhaps didn't expect that his own assassination would be just 57 days after that of his lifelong friend and colleague, Falcone.

Around the time that I was reading about Emanuela's murder there was a documentary-drama broadcast on Rai Uno about the 57 days between the two murders, called "*I 57 giorni di Paolo Borsellino*" (the 57 days of Paolo Borsellino), with Luca Zingaretti (yes, Montalbano himself) playing the part of Borsellino (in fact, for the Montalbano fanatics amongst you, if you look closely behind Montalbano's desk in his office, you will see framed pictures of Falcone and Borsellino on the wall, and I shouldn't need to mention the dramatic finale of the second series of *Young Montalbano* when the murder of Falcone is so powerfully portrayed and results in Montalbano changing his mind about moving to Genoa to live with his fiancé Livia, and instead remaining in Sicily to fight the *mafiosi*). When I watched "*I 57 giorni di Paolo Borsellino*", I'm not exaggerating when I say that I have never been so struck and so moved by a piece of television drama before. Perhaps it was because I had been doing so much reading about the circumstances prior to watching it, and I knew that a local girl was caught up in it all, but nevertheless, it was tremendously powerful. And it made me think that despite the Mafia, and other crime organisations that are considered the scourge of Italy, there are true heroes out there who are trying to battle against them in a way that I know for sure

I would never be brave enough to do.

Another one of these modern-day heroes that may be familiar to many is Roberto Saviano. Saviano wrote *Gomorrah*, which was subsequently made into an internationally acclaimed film and television series. The book - and the film - are set in and around Naples and focuses on the nefarious activities of the Neapolitan Mafia known as the Camorra. The book, while written as a novel, is based on true events that took place, including the naming of some of the key figures in the Camorra organisation. Saviano knew perfectly well that there could be a potentially fatal backlash from those he was writing about. He was forced to go into hiding soon after the book was published in 2006, around his 27th birthday, because of the number of death threats he received from senior figures in the Camorra. He still lives in an undisclosed location, most likely somewhere outside Italy, and is under 24-hour police protection.

Saviano is considered the most outspoken (and bravest) critic of organised crime in Italy. He is particularly critical of the Mafia culture that still thrives in certain parts of the country, despite the State's attempts to combat it. Saviano continues to write and campaign against the Mafia and is a very high-profile figure over here. He can be seen on various television programmes, continuing the fight against what he - and millions of others - consider to be the poisoned affliction of Italy that continues to damage the country.

Roberto Saviano is also recognised internationally. In 2008, he received the support of six Nobel Prize winners (Dario Fo, Mikhail Gorbachev, Desmond Tutu, Orhan Pamuk, Günter Grass and Rita Levi-Montalcini) who declared to the Italian Government that Saviano deserved to receive continued police protection (there have always been arguments that his protection should come to an end), and highlighted that organised crime should be a concern of all citizens in a democracy, and not only to writers such as Saviano. To say that Saviano has guts is a complete understatement. His level of courage, defiance and sheer bloody mindedness goes way beyond the norm. He has sacrificed a normal way of life in order to take on the Mafia and that deserves admiration and gratitude from all Italians.

Living in Cagliari I don't see much evidence of a Mafia culture, though I'm fairly sure some level of organised crime will exist in some shape or form, just like in most fairly large cities, not just in Italy, but also in the UK and elsewhere. It's certainly a lot more hidden and underground in Cagliari compared to how it is in Sicily, Naples and other parts around Italy (for example, in Calabria the 'Ndràngheta are notorious as a Mafia-like organisation).

I remember Adriano (yes, the very same "I'm Adriano" from Chapter 22) telling me of what happened to him and his family when they went to

Sicily on holiday several years ago. They stopped for a night in a *pensione* (like a Bed and Breakfast) in a small village in the south-western coast of Sicily. When they got up the next morning they went to where they had parked their car and all four wheels had been removed and replaced with bricks. They went back into the *pensione* and told the landlady what had happened. She just nodded knowingly and said to go into the butchers across the road and ask in there for the wheels to be returned. They went to the butchers and explained that they were staying in the *pensione* but the wheels of their car had been removed during the night. The butcher made a telephone call and they were asked to meet someone in the bar who would be able to help them out. After a 10-minute grilling in which Adriano's father was asked various questions about where they were from, why they were in Sicily, and what their intentions were for the coming days, the wheels were eventually returned half an hour later. I can't imagine the same thing happening in Sardinia.

Instead, in Sardinia, up until the 1980s at least, there was a culture of kidnapping. The kidnapping came to an end decades ago, but for some reason many people I meet in the UK (usually of a certain age) always associate Sardinia with bandits and kidnapping. It reached its height in the 1970s when it became more frequent, but even then, it wasn't happening every week, or even every month. Gangs, usually from the Barbagia area of Sardinia (right in the middle of the island) would kidnap the sons or daughters of rich barons or entrepreneurs and take them into hiding in the remote hills and mountains of Barbagia. They would demand a ransom and, upon payment, the children were returned usually unharmed (at least physically, if not emotionally). The most high-profile case, and the most recent, involved Silvia Melis, who was kidnapped in February 1997 from Tortoli, near Nuoro, and endured an abduction of 265 days. She eventually managed to escape from her captors by herself in November of the same year, and thus no ransom was ever paid.

Afterwards, however, it was revealed that payments were made by her father to middle men (including a judge and a Sardinian entrepreneur) who were involved in the negotiations with the kidnappers. It was insinuated that the payments were never passed onto the kidnappers and an investigation took place (one of the appointed investigators was a young magistrate - Antonio Ingroia - who had worked alongside Falcone and Borsellino in Palermo). Tragically, one of the supposed middle men (or negotiators) took his own life after being grilled by the investigators, and even though no-one has ever been condemned for having extorted money from the family, there remains the lingering doubt about what happened exactly in the kidnapping and liberation of Silvia Melis. Nevertheless, the kidnaps seemed to stop after that. And even then, that was the first to have occurred in around 5 years.

Anyway, to return to the subject of *Il Ponte di Emanuela Loi*, the Bridge spans the 554, which takes you out towards the coastline, where it's possible to reach the glorious beaches of *Villasimius*, *Costa Rei* and the *Sarrabus* area. Twenty years ago, when I first visited Sardinia, the only way you could reach this part of the island was via a twisty, bendy, windy (you get the idea) single lane each way road, that while beautiful and offering some of the most stunning scenery you will see on the island, would give me travel sickness every time we travelled it (nothing at all, I hasten to add, to do with the very careful and composed driving style of my father-in-law).

This road, now known as "*la vecchia cento venti cinque*" (the old 125), stretches for around 60km from just outside Cagliari and takes you to Muravera. It is certainly worth a drive if you ever find yourself in this neck of the woods. The road is mountainous and takes you through woodland and the *Monte dei Sette Fratelli* (the Mountain of the Seven Brothers) and is really spectacular. Unfortunately, there are a number of fatal accidents on the road, usually involving motorcyclists who are enjoying the thrills of the countless bends and the surrounding scenery. The theory seems to be that the motorcyclists are indulging in both at the same time and, in a momentary lapse of concentration, end up down the gorge and several hundred metres below. You do have to keep your wits about you when driving this road. It is not for the fainthearted. In fact, the fainthearted is usually quite happy sitting in the passenger's seat during this particular journey.

The road is now known as the **old** 125 because, since 2000, they started to build a split-new super highway that covers the same route, more or less, but without the countless bends. This is the **new** 125, or as the locals simply call it, *la strada nuova* - the new road. The road, while nowhere near as beautiful, is certainly more straightforward than using the old road. Instead of having to keep your wits about you while negotiating numerous bends, you have the pleasure (if you like that sort of thing) of driving through just as many tunnels. In building the new road, the engineers just bulldozed their way through any natural obstacles that were put in their path, that has resulted in a road with an abnormal number of tunnels. It seems as if you're spending more time inside the tunnels than outside. That's unlikely to be true but there's probably not much in it. I counted 17 tunnels for a stretch of 54 kilometres one day, and some of these tunnels can be 2 or 3km long.

However, this being in Italy, there has been the ubiquitous scandal associated with the building of *la strada nuova*. The scandal of *la strada nuova* is not only related to the fact that it took almost 15 years to complete, but also there have been several construction problems that have resulted in the closure of some parts of the road that have only been built in the last few years. Some stretches have been completely closed (i.e. not even reduced to one lane) for emergency repair work as the road has collapsed at certain points. The story of the construction of *la strada nuova* is certainly controversial, and has resulted in public outrage, and (eventually) a legal process against some of the major players involved, that is still ongoing. Rumours have it that at the heart of the problems of *la strada nuova* lie tales of corruption, fraud and *mazzette* (i.e. backhanders). Specifically, that the construction of some stretches of the road went to a contractor that clearly was not qualified to carry out the work properly. Of course, these are only rumours. Who am I to say? I'm not Roberto Saviano. Or Giovanni Falcone. Or Paolo Borsellino. Or Emanuela Loi.

CHAPTER TWENTY-FIVE

Sagra

The first of May is a very special day in Sardinia. It seems like the whole island converges in the city centre of Cagliari to celebrate *la Festa di Sant'Efisio*, which is also sometimes referred to as *la Sagra di Sant'Efisio*. There are hundreds of *sagra* all over Sardinia, all year round, but they all live in the shadow of *la Sagra di Sant'Efisio*.

What is a *sagra*, you may (or may not) be wondering? It's very difficult to give you a proper idea of a *sagra* until you actually experience one for yourself. Most people would translate *sagra* as "festival" or "celebration", but that doesn't truly do the *sagra* any justice. Let's say that it is like a pretty mad Gala Day, only on a much grander scale and usually (though not always) with quite serious religious overtones.

The *Festa di Sant'Efisio* is quite outrageously and unashamedly religious. As I write this, it is now in its 362nd year, having started in 1656 to celebrate Saint Efisio who Sardinians believe saved the island from the Plague in the 17th century after praying to him for salvation.

Efisio was born sometime around the mid-3rd century and was executed in 303AD in Nora, just along the coast from Cagliari. He was beheaded for disobeying the orders of the Roman Emperor Diocletian, who sent Efisio to Sardinia to persecute the Christians on the island. Instead he found the people to be friendly and welcoming to him, and he converted to Christianity after having a religious apparition. He ended up defending the local people against the persecutors.

Legend has it that, before being beheaded, Efisio prayed aloud to God to protect the Cagliari people from all those who want to oppress them purely on the basis of their faith, and to protect them from anything that might afflict them. When Cagliari was struck by the Plague in the 17th century, the local people prayed to Saint Efisio to help them and they believed their prayers were answered when the disease was driven out without too many casualties. Thus began the *Festa di Sant'Efisio*: a religious pilgrimage from Cagliari to Nora - 40km away - to demonstrate their gratitude towards the

Saint.

The procession has become gradually bigger and bigger in the 360 years that it has been celebrated, so you can imagine the size of it now. Even though nowadays the festivities associated with the *Festa di Sant'Efisio* officially go on for 4 days (from the 1st-4th May), the main event is always the 3-hour long procession that starts from the centre of Cagliari on the morning of the 1st May - regardless of the day of the week, it is always done on the 1st May - and is enjoyed by tens of thousands of spectators. The procession involves religious figures just as it did 360 years ago, but also various folk groups from all over Sardinia who are dressed in the traditional costume of their area (each area has a unique style and is very flamboyant), as well as elegantly-dressed riders on horseback, musicians (playing the launeddas), bulls, and various other participants - around 6,000 in total (that's just those taking part in the procession).

At the end of the procession, when the clock strikes 12 noon in the ancient church right in the centre of Cagliari (the church is called *la Chiesa di Sant'Efisio*, and its foundations date back to the 13th century), the bells ring out and it signals that the time is ready for the Saint to make an appearance. Although by the time he leaves the church it is always much later than 12 noon - even the Saint is not great at time keeping over here.

When I say he makes an appearance, I do of

course mean a wax model of the Saint, which is carried on a bull-drawn cart. The bulls themselves are even dressed for the occasion, decorated with flowers and gaudy colours. On top of the cart there is a glass carriage, almost like a mini-sized popemobile, where the Saint is placed on top of a plinth, with one of its (his) hands raised, almost as if it (he) is saluting the throngs. As it passes, rose petals are thrown from the windows above and the tens of thousands who line the streets begin to clap. Does it sound bizarre? It is. Very. But at the same time, it is strangely intoxicating, and quite moving.

The procession advances through the centre of Cagliari and continues on to Nora, a distance of around 40km (25 miles), where the Saint is placed in another Church (also called *la Chiesa di Sant'Efisio*) for 3 days, until the pilgrimage does the reverse journey back to Cagliari on the 4th May in order to return Saint Efisio to his rightful place in the Cagliari church.

The *Festa di Sant'Efisio* is the biggest and oldest religious procession in all of Italy, and one of the biggest in Europe, and as you might imagine, is a massive event over here. Thousands come from all over the world purely to participate and indulge in the festivities. It's so big that upon discovering that my brother's birthday is the 1st May, Flavio said to me with a straight face (probably joking, though you can never tell with him as he does it so well), "*so what's your brother's name then? Efisio?*"

As I said above, there are loads of *sagra* all over

Sardinia, all for different reasons. There is *la Sagra del Vino* (wine), *la Sagra delle Ciliegie* (cherries), *la Sagra del Pane* (bread), *la Sagra del Pesce* (fish), *la Sagra della Lumaca* (snails), and even *la Sagra dell'Anguilla* (eels). The list is endless. Most of them are celebrated in the summer to attract tourists, but in fact there are *sagra* all year round.

Our favourite is *la Sagra degli Agrumi* (the citrus fruits), that I briefly mentioned in Cibo (Chapter 13). The *Sagra degli Agrumi* takes place in Muravera, just 2km from San Vito, usually the weekend after Easter, to mark the end of the orange and lemon season. Again, there are lots of events that take place during the weekend, for example, visiting the orange groves, and exhibitions and so on, however, the main event of the festival is the two-hour procession that parades through the centre of Muravera on the Sunday.

Now I've been to quite a few Gala Days in Scotland. I've even been to two of them that are considered to be particularly special, to the extent that locals would certainly frown upon me (and probably give me a good kicking) for referring to them as Gala Days – namely Lanark's Lanimer Day and the Jethart Callant's Festival in Jedburgh. However, these are nothing compared to the main event of the *Sagra degli Agrumi* or even the *Festa di Sant'Efisio*. What they offer over here is another experience entirely. There are three aspects of the *Sagra degli Agrumi* that are especially noteworthy and that make them distinctive from anything I've ever seen in the UK.

Firstly, the traditional costumes that are worn by the parade participants, and in particular the women. I could write a separate book on the traditional Sardinian costume, and in fact many people have done, but to try to summarise, the costumes are very elaborate and extravagant affairs, usually consisting of six elements: some kind of **headgear**, like a scarf or a shawl, or a bonnet; a **blouse** with ruffles and embroidered; a **petticoat**; a **jacket or coat** decorated with silver buttons; a **skirt**, usually long and flowing and accompanied by a pinafore; and finally the black, shiny **shoes** decorated with silver buckles.

The costume is mostly a mix of reds and blacks apart from the white blouse and is embroidered delicately with intricate designs and lace. Although this depends on the area of Sardinia that the costume has been made. Each area has its own particular design. Some have green as the prominent colour, for example, or even yellow or purple. Now I may be biased when I say that the Sardinian women are beautiful – I did marry one after all – however, when you see them parading past in these amazing costumes it is difficult to say anything different. And I'm not alone in this opinion.

Paolo Mantegazza, an Italian writer from the mainland who went to visit Sardinia in the 1970s wrote the following description in his book "*The physiology of the woman*" in which he depicts the characteristics of the Sardinian women's clothing habits: *"there was a lot of head covering and an infinite grace leaving more to the imagination than to sight, and then there was the beautiful beauty of the breast. It was all a strategy of bundles, shirts and laces. All an exercise of barriers through which the profane eyes were not allowed even a glance"*. He goes on to describe the silhouette of the Sardinian woman in general terms as "an elegant, slim body, with an oval shaped, pallid face, and big eyes and an abundant breast". Well, it's difficult to argue with that!

The second aspect of the procession, though not exclusive to the *Sagra degli Agrumi* is the presence of the Mamuthones. I've just failed miserably trying to give an adequate description of the Sardinian traditional costume so God only knows how I'm going to try and give a reasonable idea of what these things are. Okay, imagine big hairy man-like beasts with an evil looking mask. Right, we're nearly there.

The Mamuthones are basically men dressed up entirely in sheep-skin or goat-skin, i.e. covered from head to toe in sheep skin, with numerous cowbells attached that make a sound with every movement. They also have a mask that looks like it has been crafted from a dead goat's head or they have a particularly evil-looking mask made especially, carved from wood by experts. They carry whips and a lasso that they use to capture the unassuming females who happen to be close by. A group of 30 or more of these Mamuthones marching in time, creating a simultaneous ringing sound from their "sheep-skin cowbells" can be quite deafening, but at the same time, is quite an enthralling and unique experience.

There is a Carnival dedicated to the Mamuthones that takes place in Mamoiada, near Nuoro in the centre of Sardinia. There's also an all-year round museum if you're really into them. I've not had the courage - I mean, the opportunity - to experience either of these yet. Maybe when I'm older. When I stop having nightmares about them.

The third feature that I must mention of the parades during the *sagra* is the elaborate nature of the "floats". The amount of work that must go into building these works of art is mind-boggling. I have seen some that have had live goats and pigs on-board and even with the *pastori* (the shepherds) roasting some *maialetto* (suckling pig) on a spit in a brick-built *caminetto* (fireplace). Some have had an orange tree growing on the float with its oranges plucked from the branches and thrown towards you (if you're lucky). All this is passing by you in a slow-moving vehicle over the course of a couple of hours. One after another. Quite remarkable. One year, in one of the floats, they actually had some *contadini* building a fireplace with bricks and cement on the float, to show you how it is done.

If you ever visit Sardinia in April, I urge you to go to the *Sagra degli Agrumi*. Despite all the lovely Gala Days you might get to see in Scotland (or elsewhere for that matter) you won't see anything like this. And why not wait until the 1st of May and combine it with the *Festa di Sant'Efisio*? It's a unique double-whammy.

CHAPTER TWENTY-SIX

La prima comunione

Last Sunday was Anna's first communion. We're only just beginning to breathe again and get back to some semblance of a normal life after several weeks of frantic preparations. *La prima comunione* is a massive event over here and the associated party that you are compelled to put on for the family afterwards is almost on the scale of a wedding. Many families decide to go to a restaurant or an *agriturismo* for the after-mass party. We decided (when I say 'we', of course I mean 'she') that we would be having it at home, which is not uncommon either, but it does involve a lot of work and preparation. We decided (again, I say 'we': what a deluded fool) to make it a little easier for ourselves by ordering the food from a well-known catering company - only the best, of course - in Cagliari. When Stefania told me how much we were spending on food, I had to ask her if we were hosting the festivities for **all** the children taking their first communion.

I didn't need to get one of Stefania's looks this time to understand why she ordered so much food and from such an overpriced (in my view, at least) caterer. The importance of doing a *bella figura* in front of your family was what was at stake here. Making sure you do a *bella figura* - it basically means making a good impression, or putting on a good show - is one of the key aspects to the communion, or any other kind of family celebration.

But it's not just the food that you have to concern yourself with. Here's a brief list of the expense that goes into putting on a first communion. Are you sitting down? Good. I'll begin. In addition to the food, there is the following: the **drinks** (alcoholic and non-alcoholic to suit all tastes, therefore, beer, white wine, red wine, soft drinks, as well as liquors: mirto, and limoncello); the **flowers** for the centre of the table as well as other **decorations** for the house; the **hair** getting done (we saved a wee bit here on my account); the **bomboniere** (like small wedding favours that are dished out at every significant event in Italy: baptism, communion, graduation, wedding and contain a little gift attached to a small bag with five sugared almonds); the **cake** (not a bog-standard £10 cake you get out of Costco - this has to be a serious, multi-decorated cake made by experts from the local *pasticceria*); the ***dolci sardi*** (Sardinian sweets that accompany the cake); the **communion dress** for Anna to be worn at the party, as well as the plain white ***vestina,*** which is the all-white religious robe that all those taking their first communion must wear, and which is complemented by a necklace with a wooden cross hanging down their fronts; **more dresses and suits**, i.e. not just for Anna but for her mum and her two brothers. I insisted my 5-year old suit still fitted me perfectly and appeared as good as new - I'd only worn it on a handful of occasions - and so there was no need. I got one of those looks again, but she seemed to accept it. She had too many other things to be worrying about; **new shoes** for everybody (I conceded on this point as I actually needed a new pair); and getting the **house cleaned** the day before and the day after the festivities.

That's not to mention all the contributions you have to make to the church for various things: for the church flowers, for the DVD they record during the ceremony, for the official photos, for the offering that they make to the poor during the mass. They should have made an offering to me after I paid for all this. I'm skint.

It was all worth it of course. We had a fabulous day and Anna loved every minute of it. It did make me think a bit during the day and reflect on the significance on what was taking place. Despite the fact that the first communion is obviously a religious ceremony and the ecumenical importance of it should not be overlooked, I do feel that the way the event is celebrated over here is almost just as much about a 'coming of age', much like Jews have with the bar (or bat) mitzvah and other cultures (religious and non-religious) will have as well. And while in Scotland there are still those who celebrate the first communion (more so in the Catholic Church it has to be said), it is not that common, and it did make me think: aside from that, what is the equivalent in Scotland? I don't think finding your first porno mag in the bushes or having your first can of cider with your mates down the park counts. Or does it? It's certainly not an act that is undertaken in full view of 50-100 members of your family, though.

Anyway, getting back to the day itself. It did begin rather inauspiciously. You have to remember that here the churches are packed, and I mean packed, especially for a first communion ceremony. The expression 'hanging from the rafters' comes to mind. The priest told the parents of all the children doing the first communion (49 children in total) not to worry, as there would be pews reserved exclusively for the parents. Only, they forgot to put signs communicating this fact to all and sundry who were looking for a seat.

Thus, Stefania entered the church to take our seats only to find that there was little space to be had. She did see a couple of spaces quite far back but a *signora* (of a certain vintage) insisted that she was keeping them for her husband and sister. Stefania knew fine well that the *signora* - and those for whom she was keeping the seats - were not parents of a communion child. Thus, she politely informed the *signora* that the pews were for the parents, but that if she moved to the side she will still have time to grab a seat, albeit with restricted viewing behind some pillars. The problem is that the verb "politely inform" does not carry much weight over here.

The *signora* held her ground: she wasn't moving. Stefania had to raise her game (and her voice a little) to insist that she move because she didn't want to be seeing her only daughter's first communion from behind a pillar, and anyway, the seats were intended for the parents. An exchange of words took place, with no immediate resolution to the problem, and then it dawned on Stefania that she recognised this *signora* from a few years previously.

When we were looking to buy a house after moving out of our apartment above the Signori Rossi, we were very interested in a house near Bar Casti (see Chapter 7). So much so that Stefania decided to visit the owner in person to negotiate a price that would be acceptable to both parties, even though the house was advertised through an estate agency. Not an uncommon thing to do, even in Scotland. I recall doing the same thing when purchasing our second home in Edinburgh, for example. However, Stefania still remembers vividly that the *signora's* initial starting point for negotiations was €40,000 above the current asking price advertised with the estate agent. All this in a culture that has no such concept as 'offers over', as was once practised in various places in the UK during the housing boom.

Needless to say, we decided not to pursue the negotiations on that occasion. But this was the kind of person we were dealing with here, in rather more pressing circumstances of finding a seat for our daughter's first communion. Luckily at that point - about 15 minutes before the start of the ceremony - the priest took to the microphone and announced to everybody that the central pews were exclusively for the parents of the children doing the first communion. We weren't the only ones having problems with ongoing negotiations.

That was the last word on the matter. You don't argue with the priest over here - especially if you are a *signora* of a certain vintage. She walked away quietly. Her tail hanging between her legs. I shouted "*nae luck, hen*", as she disappeared off, searching (in vain, I secretly hoped) for another seat. I don't think she understood me, or if she did, she didn't do me the courtesy of a reply.

Thankfully, after all the toing and froing beforehand, the ceremony proceeded quietly and without rancour (at least on my part), and was quite emotional for all concerned. After mass, everyone spilled out into the piazza in front of the church where, amidst the blazing sunshine, people were taking photographs, giving *baci*, and exchanging *'auguri'*. *Auguri*, in other words, best wishes or congratulations, are not only offered to the child taking the first communion, but protocol is also to do so to both parents. Usually in the form of *baci* on each cheek. I wasn't complaining. Generally, there was a very happy, relaxed and joyous atmosphere. At least for most people. At one point, I could overhear the *signora* still complaining about the seating arrangements to anyone who would listen (no-one I guessed), and how they should really put signs up to indicate which pews are for parents and which are for other guests. She'll be on about that for the next year probably. In between trying to sell her house.

The following day – the Monday – all the children and their families returned to the church for the 'second communion'. I'm not joking. At 5pm there was another mass, where the children take communion for the 2nd time. Afterwards there was a *festa* in the church hall, where all the families bring along the leftovers from the previous day's festivities to share around.

As I entered the church hall for the party, all the stress of the weeks prior to preparing and hosting the communion party was now a distant memory. The party was a huge success, everyone enjoyed themselves, and Stefania and – more importantly – Anna were delighted with how it had all gone. It was time to relax and rest on one's laurels of a job well done. I had no idea of what was awaiting me in the church hall.

In Italy, the game of *billiardino* or table football (sometimes even referred to in some quarters as 'babifoot' or 'foosball') is immensely popular. It has been played by men and women in Italy, of all ages, for several generations. It's played in bars, youth clubs, recreational centres, even in homes, and yes, also in church halls. I think it's fair to say that the game doesn't hold quite the same status in Scotland. Table football is nowhere near being part of the national consciousness in Scotland, or even in the UK, as it is over here. Thus, need I add, the obvious consequence of this is that the skill level of the average *billiardino* player in Scotland is way below the average *billiardino* player in Italy. It's like the Champions League against the local Sunday League. This fact was soon to be put under the spotlight in the most nerve-wracking of circumstances.

The dads were having a few 'innocent' games of *billiardino* in the church hall. One of the dads - Giovanni - called me over. I know Giovanni quite well but not well enough for him to know that I am completely shite at *billiardino* (as standards go over here ... actually I'm a regional champion in Scotland). Giovanni ignored my protestations ("*Scusa ma io non sono bravo, non gioco molto spesso*") and insisted that I play ("*Ma non importa. Dai che vinciamo*"). I had no idea what I was letting myself in for.

I discovered afterwards that Giovanni and three of the other dads had a long history of playing *billiardino* in the church hall, even dating back to childhood. Their matches were legendary. The problem (for me) was that Giovanni had decided that I would substitute his usual partner, who for some reason wasn't present, in another one of these grudge matches. Thus, I was being projected into this highly competitive environment, and forced to play a game at which my skills could be considered, at the very most, mediocre. I had to raise my game.

The game started off quietly enough. In fact, at the beginning it was only the four of us playing that were present. Giovanni had instructed me to play in defence (i.e. the goalkeeper and the defenders) while he would play his usual position in attack. The usual format is to play the best of 3 matches: with each match won by the team who is first to score 11 goals (I have no idea why it's 11: there must be championship rules somewhere that I am unaware of). However, you must win by two goals to secure a match, i.e. 11-10 is no use. The game continues until you win by two clear goals.

We won the first match 11-8, despite some very dodgy defending and risible goalkeeping errors. Giovanni was phenomenal. Every time the ball got to one of his players, he would flick his wrist in a flash, and the ball would be in the net. I'd never witnessed this level of *billiardino* playing before. I quickly realised that my objective here was just to ensure that, when I had the ball, all I had to do was somehow get it to one of Giovanni's players.

The second match went to our opponents: 11-7. I could see that Giovanni was getting a little more agitated at my poor defending, though at this point, he never said anything out loud. This was soon to change. The third and deciding match was crucial. By this time a small crowd had gathered. There must have been around 20 people swarmed around the *billiardino* table. Giovanni's shouts and exclamations drew a bit of attention from the general public, who had slowly made their way over.

We started off the third match rather shakily again. We were losing heavily. This time Giovanni wasn't holding back. He was using words that I wasn't familiar with, though it was fairly easy to guess what he was saying. It was probably along the lines of, "For fuck's sake. What are you doing you fucking clown?". Sweat was running down my brow. My heart was beating fast, as if I'd just run a half-marathon in under an hour. I was palpitating. I had never been so stressed in all the years we had been living here. Forget work, forget trying to look after three children, forget paying bills or even dealing with dangerous drivers. This was real stress.

Luckily, Giovanni went on a hot streak of goals and managed to get us back in the game. We had pulled it back to 9-7 - advantage still to them. Then

10-8. Another goal and the match - and the glory - was theirs. One more goal to them and it was all over. I could see that Giovanni was getting even more agitated.

I started whispering to myself. Concentrate Fraser. Keep your eye on the ball. Don't let them score. Keep your wits about you. Don't be distracted. I don't know how I managed it but I started to pull off some remarkable saves. Giovanni continued his extraordinary ability to score goals out of nothing and brought it back to 10-10. It would have to go to two clear goals to decide the match.

I looked around. There were a lot more people following the game now. Maybe around 50-100 people. There were even some standing on the plastic chairs that surround the church hall. The atmosphere was febrile. There were those supporting us, and another group supporting the other team. It was reaching fever pitch. I had never experienced anything like it. There were people pointing at me and saying "Is that not the Scottish guy? Why is he playing?". I even thought I heard someone say, "He's not that bad for being a foreigner", but that may have been my deluded imagination.

Another goal each and it was 11-11. Then, in quick succession, Giovanni scored another two goals. 13-11. Victory was ours. The crowd supporting our team all cheered. Giovanni turned to me and gave me a huge hug. We had done it. We had won. I couldn't believe it. I hadn't had a feeling like it for years. Relief was written all over my face. Luca was watching from the sides. He came over to me and gave me a cuddle. "I'm so proud of you, Daddy. You were brilliant." He'd never said anything like that to me before. I was trying to take it all in. People were coming up to me shaking my hand. "Bravo, bravo". And all this over a wee silly game of *billiardino*.

When we arrived home and we were reflecting on the game (I couldn't stop talking about it), Stefania explained to me that it wasn't a wee silly game of *billiardino*. It's taken seriously over here. It was important, she said, did you not see everyone watching? And then she asked me, surely there must be something in Scotland that would be similar. What would it be? I couldn't answer. Maybe an annual game of golf with your mates from childhood? A long running game of five-a-sides with the same teams? A weekly game of cards with family or friends? I couldn't think. To be honest, I couldn't care less. I was just basking in the glory of winning a game of *billiardino*. When's the next first communion? Bring it on...

CHAPTER TWENTY-SEVEN

Controlli

ontrolli (checks) are done constantly in Italy. And most of the time these *controlli* are executed in order to make sure you are who you claim you are. By law, you must always carry around with you some form of identity, usually your Identity Card (*Carta d'Identità*), or if you happen to be a johnny foreigner and you don't have one, then you must have your passport or driving licence with you at all times. For the first 3 years of living here (i.e. before I got my own *Carta d'Identità*), this was a habit that I was just not used to, and I had to be constantly reminded to take my passport with me, even if I was just popping out to the corner shop for a loaf of bread and a pint (sorry, a litre) of milk.

It is common to see the *Carabinieri* standing aside their stationary car, stopping cars randomly as they pass by and asking to see the relevant documents. I've been stopped about five or six times in the few years I've been living here. Luckily, I have always had my driving licence with me on these occasions, and my documents have always been in order (i.e. insurance and the Italian equivalent of the MOT). However, there have been plenty of times when I've been out and about and I haven't had either my licence or my passport with me. I've just been fortunate that I haven't been stopped on those occasions.

When the *Carabinieri* stop you, they take your documents away with them back to their patrol car for about 10 minutes – God only knows what they're doing: maybe checking against some database somewhere to make sure I'm not on some Interpol list, I don't know. Then they return to your car, hand you your documents, and say *"Grazie"*, as if there has been no inconvenience at all at being stopped and asked to hang around for 10 minutes, wondering anxiously at whatever you've done wrong.

I do wonder at the efficiency of doing all these *controlli*, though given how often they do them, it must be the case that they catch a lot of people out, either those who don't have insurance or those whose documents are not in order. Or maybe it's got nothing to do with that. Maybe they just do it to entertain themselves.

A few years ago, I went on a journey from Brescia to Salò that took me on a route involving countless tunnels, which reminded me of *la strada nuova*, only this time the road was on the mainland in Italy, in the north. I don't know what it is about Italians and tunnels but they do seem to like them. Maybe it's just the peculiarity of the landscape that they have to build so many. They cannot appear to find any other way around the natural, environmental obstacles, and therefore decide to just bulldoze their way through them.

Anyway, I had to embark on this particular journey from Brescia to Salò as part of a longer journey to get to Bressanone, in order to attend a Conference. Bressanone - a charming, picturesque little town - is in Trentino-Alto Adige, the region of Italy that is one of the furthest north, and borders with Austria. Bressanone is literally only a few kilometres from the Austrian border. In fact, the area of Alto-Adige used to be part of Austria before the Second World War, and was only annexed to Italy as part of the peace plan at the end of the war, where the Austrians lost and the Italians (after a tactical switch late on) were on the winning team.

Thus, a lot of the locals still consider themselves Austrian, rather than Italian, and the main language in the area is German rather than Italian. This results in the town having more of a Germanic feel to it, not just because of the language being spoken, but also in terms of the architecture and the ambience. It felt completely different from Sardinia: like being in two entirely contrasting places, even though both are in the same country. Indeed, Bressanone is about as far away as you can get from Cagliari, but still be part of Italy.

I loved it. Bressanone is dwarfed by the Dolomites, and some of the little mountain villages around Bressanone are spectacular. To get there I had to fly to Brescia, that is situated somewhere between Milan and Verona, and hire a car that would take me from Brescia all the way up to Bressanone, alongside the western side of Lake Garda. As I said, the road from Brescia to Salò took me through several tunnels. But not only that, the road passed through one of the most amazing landscapes you will encounter in all of Italy. It was green and mountainous, with rivers, lakes and trees and waterfalls and many other beautiful aspects. It reminded me of the Highlands of Scotland and I felt at home. I thoroughly enjoyed the drive, even more so because of the distraction of something strange that happened on the road that eventually resulted in giving me a wee laugh at the expense of others. A wee dollop of *schadenfreude*, as it were (well, I was heading for the German-speaking part of Italy after all).

Near the beginning of my journey, I noticed a little Fiat 500 car (a *cinquecento* to give it its proper name), and I mean an original Fiat 500 from the 1960s, not the updated, bastardised version that has recently emerged, or indeed its ugly namesake that was built in the 1980s, that shared absolutely nothing with the original 500, apart from the name.

Now, I'm no Jeremy Clarkson (thank God); in fact, I know next to nothing about cars. When people ask me what kind of car such and such has (if they know I've had a ride with them), my reply usually revolves around what colour it was, not the make, as I wouldn't have a clue what make it was. However, I can recognise the aesthetic beauty of the old Fiat 500 car and appreciate its wonder. It is the epitome of cool. Especially in winter, as there's no heating ventilation in them.

To get back to my story, I noticed one of these little beauties on the road, and as I overtook it, I spotted another one just ahead. Then, as the road stretched out before me at one point, I could see about 100 of them spread out over about 5km of otherwise empty road - a long, winding snake of Fiat 500 cars. It was a sight to behold. Basically, it was one of these Sunday events that seem to take place with car lovers where they all get together somewhere and decide to drive from A to B in convoy. I've seen them in the UK as well, though usually with classic cars and certainly not in a group with as many as I could see on this journey. There were loads of them. And as I've highlighted elsewhere (Chapter 23), the Italians do like to indulge in their convoys.

Anyway, at one point I could see an impending *Carabinieri* road-check. Need I elucidate further? Yes, the bastards (or comic geniuses, depending on the way you look at it) decided to flag down one of the convoy in order to carry out one of their standard document checks.

This put the whole convoy operation into crisis. What do we do? Do we stop and wait at the side of the road? Do we continue on and hope he/she catches up? They knew fine well that the latter option would be foolish, as far as their neat convoy was concerned, as these checks can last anything up to 10-15 minutes. As I looked in my rear-view mirror, I started to see one, then two, then several others having to pull into the side of the road. They must have taken up about a mile of hard shoulder, causing chaos for all around, as it wasn't even a proper motorway.

I just drove on, giggling away to myself like the immature little *schadenfreude*-lover that I am, imagining the scene as they tried to start up again. They would've had to have waited for an unlikely gap of several minutes in the traffic before trying to get back on the road again with their neat convoy. I started picturing them all still waiting there at the side of the road at midnight, pitch-black darkness all around, *"right comrades, let's try now. I think we can do it this time"*. It must have been a long day that one. And all because of the *Carabinieri*.

I did promise in an earlier chapter that I would attempt to explain the difference between the *Carabinieri* and the *Polizia*. I wish I hadn't. I'm still not sure, but then neither is the general public over here. I get various different answers to this question. I believe the formal difference is that the *Carabinieri* form part of the military, while the *Polizia* are more like what is usually understood by the Police, that is, being linked to the State. However, I was told rather sagely by someone that, despite this, they both have the same role: i.e. to keep the country and its subjects safe. And this means that their roles often overlap. For example, they could be investigating the same murder case.

Another view that I have heard is that if you have done something wrong and start to run away, the *Polizia* will chase you but the *Carabinieri* will shoot you. I think (yes, I think) this was a joke. Another thing is that the *Carabinieri* are always the butt of the usual "stupidity" jokes. In the same way that the Irish (or famous footballers, like David Beckham for example) are targeted in the UK[8]. Similarly, the people from Liguria (i.e. the city of Genoa and around) are targeted for being mean just like the Scots are in the UK. Of course, it's all nonsense, but I have to admit to laughing away at some of the *Carabinieri* jokes when they're recounted to me. Usually I laugh a little bit louder than others, just to confirm to the doubters that I have understood the joke.

---

[8] if you know your football you might (I say, "might") be interested to know that Francesco Totti, the iconic Roma player, is targeted over here in the same way as David Beckham is in the UK - quite unfairly I might add, for both of them. I would like to highlight to their lawyers that they are both highly intelligent human beings.

The other *controllo* over here is related to your residency – where do you claim you live. This is all very complicated and long-winded as there are certain advantages (or disadvantages, depending on the way you look at it) one can gain related to where you claim your residency is. Thus, when you go to the local *Comune* (Town Hall) and sign a form saying you are now living at say, via Roma, 48, the officials from the *Comune* will come round to your house one day, unannounced, just to make sure you do actually live there. If you're out (maybe to pop out to the shop, but you are stopped by the *Carabinieri* to check your documents so you're out a bit longer than you intended), don't worry. The officials from the *Comune* will come back another day and check again.

I do wonder at the resources that are expended with all these checks and controls. It must serve some kind of purpose, but I'm just not convinced of the value of it yet. Stefania lived in the UK for more than 10 years and never had the need to officially declare her residency there. She was able to work, have a bank account, vote, and do many other things without the need to formally declare that she was living permanently in the UK or have anyone come round to where she was claiming she lived to make sure that she did indeed live there. Instead, I was unable to do any of those things until I officially signed myself up as being resident in Italy, proving that I was semi-rich (see Chapter 16) (irony alert) and waiting until it was checked that I was actually telling the truth. I couldn't honestly tell you how many times I have had to have my identity checked by the *Carabinieri*, or been put on the spot to produce documents to prove who I am. It's countless.

It's as if they're all just having a laugh at my expense. Those *schadenfreude*-loving bastards. Maybe they're just getting their own back after all the jokes that are made against them for being stupid. I should just get on with it, and accept that they're comic geniuses.

CHAPTER TWENTY-EIGHT

Birra, pizza e caffè

Like many of my fellow countrymen, I do like a drink. I cannot deny it. Therefore, it's been a pleasure to explore the various alcoholic drinks that are on offer here since moving to Sardinia.

Probably the most distinctive Sardinian liquor, that is undeniably from the island, is *mirto*. *Mirto* is like *limoncello*, only it is purple in colour and is made from myrtle berries rather than lemons. It's usually consumed at the end of a long meal, accompanied by a coffee, and is served directly from the freezer. It is very sweet and goes down easily. Sometimes too easily. It's not unknown for Flavio and I to make our way through a bottle of it in an evening. And then suffer the morning after. And there's no Irn Bru to help with the hangover either.

They do have some nice beers too: the main Sardinian beer is called *Ichnusa*. *Ichnusa* was the name given to the island by the ancient Nuragic civilisations that lived here around 2000BC. It actually means "footprint", as legend has it that the land mass of Sardinia is the footprint that the Gods left in hopping between Europe and Africa. *Ichnusa* is a lovely, light beer that can be found everywhere, in bottles and in draught. I drink it a lot. Just to support the local economy.

There are also some delicious beers produced by the local micro-breweries (called *birrificio*). The *Birrificio di Cagliari* is situated in a rather non-salubrious location on the outskirts of Cagliari, in amongst some other industrial buildings, but the beer that they make on the premises is as palatable and fresh-tasting as you'll find anywhere. And you can eat there as well. It's almost always packed out and booking ahead is essential.

When you order draught beer over here, you need to know some parlance. Because of the metric system, there is no such thing as a pint or a half pint. The nearest equivalent to a pint is 0.40 litres - known as a *zero quaranta* - and for a half-pint you have to ask for a *zero venti* - that is, 0.20 litres.

Stefania still recalls when she first walked into a pub in England and asked the barman for a "zero twenty". The guy didn't have a clue what she was talking about, of course, and probably thought he was the victim of some kind of elaborate student prank. To make matters worse, she felt she would be better understood if she elaborated and asked for a "clear zero twenty", which she had translated directly from the Italian "*birra chiara*", meaning a lager. It's important to get the language right. This is serious stuff we're talking about here.

I've said in another chapter, and I think it would be churlish to argue against it, in Scotland we do tend to have a culture that revolves around drinking and going to the pub, which contrasts with the Italian culture that I experience over here. While the Italians do enjoy a drink, it has to be said that it is more often than not accompanied by food. And, the result is, they perhaps don't drink quite as much as we do.

I still remember on my first visit to Sardinia when we went for a night out with Stefania's friends to the Italian equivalent of a pub. We ordered up some beers and after half-an-hour I had dutifully finished my zero forty glass, only to look around and see about an inch of beer had been drunk from all the others at the table. I didn't know what to do. I asked the guy next to me, who I knew spoke quite good English, whose round it was, and he just looked at me bewildered. "*What's a round?*", he asked me. The concept just doesn't exist. They nursed those pints all night. It brings a whole new meaning to the expression, "going out for a pint".

Indeed, one of the first things I noticed over here

was that, in place of our often-used expression "Why don't we meet up for a pint?", Italians will often say, "*magari ci vediamo per una pizza?*". The pizza replaces the pint of beer as the cultural focal point of social gathering. In fact, at the end of the academic year it is commonly the case that there will be a *pizzata* organised for the class of your child (basically meeting up in a pizzeria for an evening), where you are expected to attend and mix with the other parents. And this doesn't only apply for the school. There will be a *pizzata* for the basketball team, the scouts, the music school, your workplace, and so on and so forth. With three children in tow, last summer we attended 8 *pizzata*, and we had to turn some down as well.

Not that I'm complaining of course. It goes without saying that the quality of pizza over here is second-to-none. The number of pizzerias is countless - and I include here the ones that do take-away only (incidentally, the best pizza in Cagliari can be found at the Oca Bianca restaurant in via Napoli, near the port... in my humble opinion!). I think the proliferation of pizzerias is similar to what the purpose and universality of fish and chip shops used to be like in the UK. In the sense that the take-away pizzeria is the first port of call for families if they don't feel like cooking a meal for an evening. And they're everywhere.

In the UK, the choice of take-away food has expanded into many other areas in recent times - Chinese, Indian, Japanese, Thai, American,

Mexican, to name but a few. But in Italy, they have still stuck to their national pride and the city is strewn - i.e. on almost every street corner - with pizzerias. And there are hardly any take-aways of the foreign variety. In fact, there are hardly any restaurants that are non-Italian. I'm not saying there are none at all. But there are very few, and proportionally, much less compared to the UK. It would appear, for the time being at least, that Italians do prefer their own cuisine before they might expand into other nationalities' delicacies.

The other food outlet you see everywhere over here is the *panificio*. Not to be confused with a baker (which would be a *pasticceria*, for those interested), the *panificio* only sells bread. Bread and bread alone. But every type of bread you could ever think of.

Italians love their bread and almost every meal will have a bread basket in the middle of the table. And thus, they tend to buy it every single day from the *panificio*. When we lived in our first flat above the Signori Rossi, there was a *panificio* on the street corner, about 70 yards from the house. It was bliss. I would toddle along mid-morning to purchase my daily portion of bread for the family and it would still be warm to the touch, and would smell delicious. It has been known (just don't tell Stefania) that a wee roll or two (or should I say, panini) might have been consumed on the short walk back to the house, as it is just impossible to resist. And there is an important point here: if it is a proper *panificio*, the bread will have been baked on the premises. If not, then it becomes a bread shop, not a *panificio*.

What Italians make of the British sliced variety that lasts about two weeks, God only knows. Actually, I do know. They think it's sacrilege. They just don't understand it. In fact, it's almost impossible to find sliced bread here in the shops. What they do sell is a horrible, long-life bread that has a use-by date of 2 or 3 months hence, which they call American Sandwich bread. It's disgusting and over-priced too. A half loaf of this bread (I've no idea why they sell it in half loaves, probably because it's so objectionable) costs about €1.25. I've yet to find fresh sliced bread in the shops, i.e. similar to what you would normally come across in the UK.

Another thing that Italians cannot survive without is, of course, *il caffè*. As you will no doubt be aware, how they drink coffee over here is very different from how we would in the UK. I'm talking specifically about the Italian habit of drinking *espresso* in a tiny cup, rather than in a large, hot, steaming mug of the watered-down variety. I do accept, however, that there has been a cultural revolution in the UK with regard to coffee drinking in recent years, where the drinking of *espresso*, *macchiato* and the like are just as, if not more, popular than drinking the traditional British instant coffee. However, that was certainly not the case 20 years ago.

When Stefania and I first met, I had no idea of espresso coffee. Remember, I grew up in Kilmarnock. Anyway, on our first date, after a few 'clear zero twenties' down the pub, Stefania invited me into her flat for a coffee. Much to my great disappointment and annoyance, she actually went into her kitchen and started to prepare it.

The problem was, she was an Italian student visiting the UK in the mid-1990s. The concept of the espresso coffee cup had not reached Great Britain at this point. She duly brought over with her from Italy her *caffettiera* (Italian coffee percolator that you put on the hob, for those just as ignorant as I was about coffee), but she didn't have the cups to serve it in. She assumed that there would be some supplied in the flat where she'd be staying. So, instead, she had to make do with large coffee mugs. Thus, when she prepared my coffee, she had to pour a tiny, espresso amount of coffee into the bottom of a large sized, British-style mug. It looked ridiculous.

When she came back into the living room and handed me my coffee, I erupted. It was probably the tension of the first date. Or maybe it was just unforgivable coffee ignorance. "WHAT THE HELL IS THIS?", I said. "IS THIS SOME KIND OF JOKE?". She just looked at me, stunned. "No, what do you mean?".

"ARE WE ON RATIONS HERE?", I asked, stupidly, merely confirming her suspicions that she had just been on a date with the culturally-aware and broad-minded equivalent of Nigel Pharage[9]. "No, that's how we drink coffee in Italy", she replied calmly, while at the same time pondering how the fuck she could usher me promptly to her door without creating too much of a scene.

Luckily, we got over it. I had to confess my sins of not knowing anything about how one should really drink coffee, and we managed to sort it all out. But it did make me think about the cultural difference. For example, I'm a great lover of malt whisky. And when I see people pouring in water (I can accept a couple of drops, but only a couple), or God forbid, lemonade or coca cola, then I probably have the same feelings of despair that Italians have when they see Brits drinking their large mugs of watered-down instant coffee. It just shouldn't be done. The whole experience is ruined.

Of course, things are rather different now. The proliferation of coffee shops all over the UK means that British people are much more aware of the joys of coffee, cappuccino, macchiato and everything else. There is a major difference though - you won't find Starbucks, Costa Coffee or Caffè Nero over here. Indeed, neither will you find Pizza Hut, Dominos or anything similar. The bars and pizzerias in Italy are all independently owned, each with their own character and identity. I understand

---

[9] Nigel Pharage was a school friend of mine who was a xenophobic arse and was wary of all things foreign. Any resemblance to the culturally broad-minded and continental-loving politician Nigel Farage is purely coincidental.

that these coffee shop conglomerates have tried to enter the Italian market but have failed miserably. Italians don't trust them. They much prefer to go to their local bar where they know the bar staff and get their coffee served in a proper ceramic cup. They're not fans of having their coffee served in a paper cup with their name branded down the side in a black marker pen. Nor do they feel the need to walk out of the bar with the coffee cup held in their hands, rushing to their next appointment.

But there's another, more pragmatic side to Italian coffee drinking habits, over and above the pleasure Italians take in drinking strong, full-tasting coffee: it's too hot most of the year to drink a big, steaming mug of coffee. You just want to get it down quickly and easily, without sweating over your piping hot beverage for ten minutes or more. It makes practical sense. I love tea but from May through to October, I just don't feel like drinking it over here. It's just too damn hot. So, I prefer to stick to my espresso coffee, made with the *caffettiera*. Poured into the bottom of a large sized mug. Just for old times' sake.

CHAPTER TWENTY-NINE

Salute!

Italians are obsessed with their health. They are also well-known to be fairly candid with others about their various ailments and afflictions. There's no doubt that health is important over here. With every get-together over a drink (only one, mind you), you will hear the exclamation of "*salute!*" as they clink their glasses, to toast each person's good health. Of course, we sometimes do that as well, but just not as often. We prefer the good old meaningless "Cheers", while guzzling it down our throats before the word has barely left our mouths.

The Italians talk constantly about their health, even with people they might not know so well. It's very similar to what we do when we talk about the weather. So, for example, you might be standing at a bus stop, and instead of exchanging banal pleasantries about the weather you might find that the *signora* next to you might comment on the terrible trouble she's having with her bunion. And the other thing they do, which is rather irritating, is try to offer their advice on whatever health problem you happen to have. They might offer a full-proof remedy, or worse, ask to see whatever it is you may have, so that they can begin a full medical consultation on the matter.

Italians are most frightened of getting a "*colpo d'aria*". Everywhere you go you hear this expression. For example, if there's someone that I know that is unwell, I'll ask them, "what happened? Why are you under the weather" (see, I'm just as obsessed about the weather). "Well, I was out last night and I got a *colpo d'aria*", they will reply, on more occasions than I'd care to count. You will hear parents shouting it at their kids at the park in the evenings, "Come here Francesco and put this fleece on. If you don't, you're going to get a *colpo d'aria*".

What is this mysterious *colpo d'aria*, you might ask. It sounds awful, doesn't it? It means being hit by air. Yes, I mean it. Being hit by air. I suppose we might translate it better as getting a draught of wind, but it is this very thing that Italians seem to be in fear of their lives of.

What many Italians do to combat this

horrendous *colpo d'aria* is to wear a *maglietta della salute*. Basically a vest. If you don't wear a *maglietta della salute*, then you're asking for trouble. Or so the theory goes. I don't wear a vest. I don't know exactly why. I suppose I associate wearing vests with Rab C Nesbitt, so I just don't feel right wearing a vest. Italians, or at least Italians of a certain age and young children, wear them all the time. And I mean, all the time.

Just the other day, I met a *signore*, probably in his mid-to-late 70s, who started to strike up conversation with me in the shop. It's been particularly hot recently: the temperature has been hovering around the 40oC mark for a couple of weeks now. After exchanging a few words about how hot it is at the moment, he then went on to tell me about his friend who has converted a cave in the mountains in the middle of Sardinia into a fully-equipped dwelling, where he escapes to from July to September in order to escape the heat.

The very amiable *signore* was saying to me that he would love to do the same, as he finds the heat so unbearable at this time of year. He started to describe in great detail what he would do exactly to make his cave comfortable. The truth is, he was starting to go on and on a bit, and my attention started to drift. It was at this point that I noticed that he had a *maglietta della salute* underneath his shirt. Along with his elegant trousers and shoes. For comparison purposes, I was wearing shorts, a short-sleeved t-shirt and a pair of sandals.

I felt I had to interrupt his discourse. "*Listen pal*", I said, "*that's all very well, and your intentions of moving to the mountains and building a cave are all very honourable. But for fuck's sake, could you not just forgo the vest when you're getting dressed in the morning? And maybe even put on a pair of shorts rather than your smart trousers? You might find that it could help you cope a little better with the heat, rather than having to move to the country for a couple of months to live in a cave. Ya daft old duffer*".

Actually, I didn't say that last part. In fact, I didn't say the first part either. Or even the bit in the middle. The truth is, I just nodded my head and pretended to listen. But I did think all those things. And at the end of our (rather one-sided) conversation, I wished him all the best in his endeavours of cave conversion, while at the same time, imagining him sitting in it having his dinner while wearing a shirt, bow tie, elegant trousers and shoes, and a dinner jacket (on top of his *maglietta della salute*, of course), bemoaning his decision to move to a cave for the summer, as it doesn't seem to have made much difference to him coping with the heat.

When you're down the beach, the general rule over here is that you have to wait at least two hours (Stefania thinks that's not even enough) after eating your lunch before you can go back in the water. The fear is that you suffer a congestion if you go back in too soon. In fact, Italians are almost as fearful of a *congestione* as they are of a *colpo d'aria*.

Thus, I have to cope with three frustrated children asking me every 5 minutes, "*can I go in now, Dad?*". Usually followed by my question, "*Is your mum watching?*", which they know is secret code for making the decision regarding whether it's ok to go back in or not.

The other thing that you find over here with regard to the obsession with health is that in order to play any sport, you have to have a medical check done to make sure that you are in a fit enough condition to cope with the sport you have decided to participate in. This is the same for young children, as it is for adults of all ages. Finn even had to do it recently as we wanted him to try a couple of lessons of swimming to see if he would like it. The officials at the swimming pool wouldn't even let him do a couple of trial lessons if he didn't have the appropriate medical certificate.

When I say, "appropriate medical certificate", what I mean is that depending on which sport you're doing, and the level you're playing at, you'll need a medical certificate that allows you to play either at a level of "*agonistico*" (best understood as "competitive") or "*non-agonistico*" (non-competitive). I play football every week including in seven-a-side tournaments, thus I need a medical certificate each year that allows me to play at an *agonistico* level. Stefania does Pilates twice a week: for her, a *non-agonistico* certificate is sufficient, which is a much less strenuous check and is much more simple and straight-forward. It is rare for anyone to fail a *non-*

agonistico check, unless they find something seriously wrong with your heart, for example. Anyway, you get the picture.

It probably goes without saying, but the certificate that allows you to participate in an *agonistico* sport requires much more thorough checks, involving (amongst other things) cycling on an exercise bike for around 15 minutes while various wires with suction pads are attached to your chest, heart and other parts of your body. Thus, you are naked from the waist up. You are told to bring a towel as it can get rather sweaty as you are tested to your limits: for example, doing the equivalent of cycling up a 45-degree hill for several minutes. Once you go through all of this, the specialist sports medic will (hopefully) sign you off as fit and healthy and you are free to go and play whatever sport it is you want. While he's laughing all the way to the bank.

One of Stefania's more senior colleagues, Elisabetta, recently went for a check for a *certificato medico*, as she had decided to take up Pilates to try and combat her gradual weight gain over the years. Elisabetta is about 6 feet tall and could probably best be described as a 'big wummin'. By the time of her interest in taking up Pilates she was approaching retirement, and hadn't done much exercise in her life up to that point. Despite the fact that the *non-agonistico* certificate would have been sufficient for doing Pilates, she was advised by a friend that she should ask for an *agonistico* certificate. Simply because the check is more thorough, and the friend felt that it might be a good idea to get a comprehensive examination before taking up some regular physical exercise.

When Elisabetta arrived at the sports clinic, she told the receptionist that she was there for an *agonistico* check. The receptionist took one look at her and said, "Are you sure, *signora*?" You don't mean a *non-agonistico* check?". Elisabetta, offended at this slight from the young, fit looking receptionist, dug her heels in even more, "No, I'm absolutely sure what I mean. I'm here for an *agonistico* check".

As the people in the crowded reception area were beginning to take an interest in the unfolding events, the receptionist called through the back, "Hey, Stefano", she shouted, "can you come here a minute? There's a *signora* out here claiming that she's here to do an *agonistico* check". Unsure at what he was expected to do or say, Stefano, the sports doctor, stifled his giggles as he looked at Elisabetta. "You do know what's involved in the *agonistico* medical test, *signora*?". "Yes, of course I do", she lied. She hadn't actually looked into it, other than knowing that it was a thorough check. She didn't know what she was in for.

To cut a long story short, Elisabetta was wired up to do the cycling test, stripped to the waist apart from her normal brassiere, and after puffing and wheezing her way through the first 5 minutes of cycling, decided she had to call it a day. The sports doctor couldn't provide her with the necessary medical certificate, and not only, wasn't even in a position to sign her off for a *non-agonistico* one either. At least not until she had gone through various other tests, so that he was able to ascertain a certain degree of health and fitness that would allow her to perform normal, non-competitive physical activity. The Pilates classes would have to wait.

The funny thing is that while Italians are obsessed about health and take these things very seriously, they are less keen to talk about money matters – an inverse relationship that we Brits might have about the two issues. I find that many Brits will happily tell you how much they paid for this, that and the other, including their house and car, perhaps even letting on how much they earn – a situation that would never occur over here. It is common to know more about your neighbour's piles in Italy than you would ever know about their approximate annual income.

In addition, Stefania highlighted to me once that she finds it remarkable that almost everyone she meets in the UK, who has a fairly decent income and a good job, are always at pains to tell her that they've grown up in a working-class family or in a council house. Something that would not be discussed so openly in Italy: no-one would admit to being from a working-class background, even if it were indeed true, and even if they were earning a decent wage and had climbed the social ladder.

I remember discussing with Signor Rossi - during one of my monthly visits downstairs - the topic of when Stefania might be returning to work after Finn was born. I told him the truth, which was that we were waiting to see if my university contract would be extended before deciding whether we could afford to have Stefania take a longer maternity leave. Otherwise, she would have to return to work sooner than we would have preferred, as we wouldn't be able to manage financially. By his reaction and facial expression, you'd have thought I'd just shared with him some intimately private information about the swelling I've recently noticed on my testicles. Although bizarrely enough, if I had shared such information, he probably would have been much more at ease with the situation. And he might even have asked to take a look. Just to see if he could offer some advice on the matter.

CHAPTER THIRTY

Festa!

I've already written about this but only because it's true. Italians like their parties. Birthdays, baptisms, first communions, confirmations, Saint days, sagras. You name it, they celebrate it. As I said in Cibo (Chapter 13), even an ordinary Sunday is marked as *festa* on the calendar. And the other thing is: they like to put in a lot of preparatory work into their *festa*. In particular, there is a lot of attention focused on what they are going to eat. As opposed to what they are going to drink.

During my first visit to Cagliari as a student – more than 20 years ago now - I still remember vividly the amount of preparation that went into the 'menu' for the get-together with Stefania's friends for Hogmanay. The night before Hogmanay, all the friends who were to be attending the *festa* came round to Stefania's house to have a 3-hour discussion about what food would need to be bought the following day for the various courses that would be prepared for the meal. There were 12 of us there and the discussion went on and on and on, as there was a difference of opinion about what would constitute the menu. At certain times I was convinced that the discussion was getting so out of hand that it could possibly come to blows. We were all in our early 20s at the time. There's wasn't anyway near as much discussion about the alcohol that was to be purchased for the party.

Italians are passionate about their food so it's not easy to reach agreement between 12 people regarding what to eat for a special occasion. But the other thing that happens in these situations, when opinions are being expressed fervently about a topic, is that everyone talks at once. The usual general rules comprising conversation just don't apply. For example, "I speak, you listen, then you speak and I listen" would be nice, but it seems to be too much for them to bear. I still recall that evening taking a step back and observing them all from a distance.

All 11 of them (i.e. myself excluded) that were sitting round the table discussing the menu for the following evening were talking simultaneously.

Each of them was trying to get their opinion over to the others, and it was felt that the best way to do this was by talking over everyone else. And as I sat back, I thought to myself, "If they're all talking at the same time, who is actually listening?" Indeed, my sole contribution to the evening of, *"Can we not just get a couple of steak pies in, for fuck's sake?"* was completely ignored, although that is not an uncommon occurrence for me.

Hogmanay, or *capodanno*, is just as much a celebration over here as it is in the UK. In fact, given that the Italians don't celebrate the world-renown Mr Fawkes on the 5th November each year (what's their problem?), *capodanno* is the one occasion in the calendar year where you can be sure that there will be plenty of fireworks.

My first *capodanno* took place in Flavio's flat right in the centre of Cagliari. After a splendid meal, worthy of all the arguments and fall outs and minor injuries that took place to organise it, the fireworks started going off all around us at midnight. Everyone was out on their balconies to observe the scene, with glasses of *spumante* in hand, shouting out New Year greetings across the streets.

The one thing that adds to the atmosphere is the deafening cacophony of car alarms simultaneously sounding out, triggered by all the fireworks going off. It makes quite a din. I did make the suggestion to my fellow guests that you would think that the car owners, who know this is going to happen on this day each year, would perhaps decide not to switch on their alarms for one day, however, again my point fell on deaf ears.

Or maybe on this occasion it was the case that my fellow guests didn't respond because they were truly deafened by the racket going on. Actually, I'm deluding myself. The truth is probably that they decided to just ignore that dull and tedious *straniero* who was evidently incapable of expressing himself clearly in Italian.

The thing I learned that Hogmanay night is that when you host a *festa* in Italy you have to make every effort to prepare the party as a sit-down meal. The notion of a cocktail party or a buffet just doesn't cut it over here. It doesn't matter if it's a fairly small affair - such as hosting 12 people for Hogmanay - or if it's for a larger festivity, like a first communion or a baptism - i.e. a *festa* that would include all the family, and potentially around 30, 40 or even 50 people. The right and proper thing to do is to get them all seated and serve up a full five course meal, almost as if they're at a wedding.

The number of hours that go into organising these events and preparing all the food, not to mention how hard you're working on the day as hosts, would be unimaginable to most British minds. Recently we went to a family *festa* to celebrate the confirmation of the son of one of Stefania's 17 cousins (we get invited rather a lot to these kinds of events because of the number of family ties we have).

Stefania's cousin and his wife live in a *villetta* (a terraced house over 3 floors), and had transformed the *cantina* (the basement) into a temporary restaurant that was able to accommodate about 15 tables all scattered around the room. There must have been around 60 or 70 guests at this *festa*. It was incredible. After I enquired about how they were able to do all this, it was explained to me that Stefania's cousin and his wife have a kind of cooperative going with their friends and neighbours that means they will help out when someone in the 'cooperative' is having one of these mega-parties, by preparing and serving the food, as if working in a restaurant. The favour is returned when you're hosting one of your own celebrations. I just cannot imagine - for one second - a similar scenario occurring in the UK.

If you're invited to a party in the UK, what do you normally take round as a gift for your host? A cake, some chocolates, a bottle of wine perhaps? Maybe even a bunch of flowers? Over here, there is a bit more flexibility regarding what you might decide to take with you as an offering.

When Stefania and I got married, a big group of my friends came over to Sardinia and rented a couple of villas along the coast from Cagliari. In the week leading up to the wedding they decided to host a party and invited Sara and Flavio along, as sister (and partner) of the bride. Just as a way of extending the hand of international friendship before the wedding day. Flavio turned up at the party with a huge bag of tomatoes as a gift for my friends, as a way of thanking them for the invitation: probably about 3 kilos worth. A not insignificant gift as they would have been enough to feed about 10 of them for several days. However, you would have thought by their reaction that he had brought along 3 kilos worth of nail clippings. Actually, nail clippings might have been of more use to them given their dietary habits on that holiday. *"Where's the beers big man?"*, I could hear them asking.

Fifteen years later and they still talk about it. They thought it was one of the funniest and most eccentric things they had ever witnessed, whereas for Sardinians, it would be a perfectly normal thing to do. Especially if you've grown the produce yourself in your own *orto*. Indeed, it would be considered an act of generosity on the part of the tomato-giver. I still get asked by some of my friends when I'm back in Scotland, *"How's Flavio getting on? How's his tomatoes?"* They seem to think that all he does is go around to people's houses offering tomatoes when he's invited to a party.

I suppose it also underlines the difference in attitudes towards food that there is between Italians and Scots. When I tell my friends in Sardinia about what happened to me a few years ago in a cafe near Pitlochry, they simply don't believe me. Mind you, neither do my friends in Scotland.

We were on holiday and were staying in a small

village in beautiful Perthshire. The village had a shop, a post office and a cafe, all part of the same building. One day we decided to have lunch in the village cafe as we had been out and about all morning and thought it might be nice to support the local economy (translation: we couldn't be bothered making our own lunch that day).

After consulting the menu, I had decided to go for 'Soup of the Day'. I do like my soup, especially home-made. The waitress replied by asking me what kind of soup I would like. A little confused by the question I replied with a question, "*you mean the chef has prepared more than one soup of the day today?*". "*No*", she said, "*you just have to go and choose a tin from the shop next door and we'll heat it through for you*". Aghast I decided to just have a pot of tea instead. I asked her if they had any cakes or biscuits to accompany my tea. "*Not a problem*", she said. I ended up leaving with the rest of the packet of chocolate digestives that I had to purchase from the shop. It was certainly a unique catering set-up they had.

Despite progress in the UK over the years, and despite the fact I know that it's really unfair to generalise (but I'm going to do it anyway), it's still undeniable that we're talking about two completely different perspectives when it comes to cooking and appreciating good food. I remember reading about Jamie Oliver's experience of visiting the south of Italy and his amazement at discovering the level of knowledge amongst young children of the different cuts of meat there are, and which ones are the most delicious, and so on. In the context of Oliver's ongoing campaign in trying to encourage young people to cook more in Britain, there was an article in the newspaper a few years ago which included an interview with a young guy who basically said that cooking, or preparing a meal, was simply a waste of his time. He explained that he just goes to the supermarket, buys a pizza and shoves it in the microwave. That would be sacrilegious over here. The habit (I could say, perhaps unfairly, that the habit is especially true amongst students - I was guilty of it myself when I was at university) of making a pot noodle or beans on toast for dinner would not even be considered for a nanosecond over here. It's just not an option.

The other thing I've noticed is how parties or social get-togethers over here are often organised on the hoof. Or, as they say here, *all'improviso*. It's not uncommon to be down the park of an evening and you might bump into some friends that you haven't seen for a while. After some friendly conversation, it might be the case that you end up going to the nearest pizzeria that evening, or organising a trip to a local *agriturismo* for the following day, if it was over the weekend. Just like that. That would never happen in Scotland, at least not in my experience. Social events are planned several months in advance. And you always need to include a contingency plan depending on what the weather will be like on the day. Not a problem in Sardinia. A barbeque will be a barbeque.

I still remember hosting a barbeque in Edinburgh many years ago, and persevering as the rain continued to fall from the sky. And I don't mean it was raining. It was absolutely pelting it down. In the end, I had to ask Stefania to come out and hold an umbrella for me while everyone else waited inside the house waiting for some rain-soaked sausages. I thought to myself, "*why am I doing this? What is the point in this?*" I'm fairly sure I'm not alone amongst my fellow Scots in experiencing this same scenario. It would have made more sense to have cooked the meat indoors but there was a stubborn, stoic side of me saying "*if you invited your friends round for a barbeque then that's what they're going to get*", even if I succumbed to hypothermia in the process. If only I'd known about the *maglietta della salute* in those days. How life could have been so very different.

CHAPTER THIRTY-ONE

Raccomandazioni

It's not that easy to find work in Italy, but especially so in the south - and that includes Sardinia. The dream ticket for everyone in this neck of the woods is trying to procure a *posto fisso*: a fixed, permanent position, usually in the public sector. Most people go from one short-term contract to another, searching (more often than not) in vain for the Holy Grail that is the *posto fisso*. There was even a comedy film that came out a couple of years ago that revolved around searching for and having a *posto fisso*. It starred the well-known Italian actor/comedian Checco Zalone entitled *Quo Vado* (Latin for 'Where do I go?'). A hilarious film, if you ever fancy a wee shot at

Italian cinema.

But it's no joke. One of the main obstacles that gets in the way of ordinary citizens finding a *posto fisso* is the culture of *raccomandazioni*. *Raccomandazioni* - literally, it means recommendations - is the practice of someone in a position of power 'recommending' someone (usually, but not always, a family member) for a job, even if the person recommended doesn't have the necessary qualifications or skills to do the job competently. You hear all kinds of stories of *raccomandazioni* all the time. Everyone has a story to tell. I've heard stories of big, well-known private organisations who would offer a job to the son or daughter of someone due for retirement in exchange for them declining the lump sum that's due to them. Even if the son or daughter will likely not have the skills for the job, and even if the organisation is preventing someone more qualified or more competent from getting a deserved chance, it does of course save the big private organisation a bit of money. Everyone involved in it benefits, so what is there to think about?

The Italians even tell jokes about the kind of corruption that goes on with *raccomandazioni*. One I heard recently is about the decision-making process regarding the allocation of work to paint the local town hall. A German painter submits an estimate of €3000, a Frenchman provides an estimate of €6000, and finally the local Italian says it will cost €9000. The mayor invites each of them to his office individually, in order to present their case. The German explains that he has a special kind of paint and so it only requires one coat, and he claims that he can obtain cheaper labour than the others, thus he can offer to do the work for such a low price of €3000. The Frenchman explains that the town hall will require at least two coats, possibly more in some places, and while he doesn't overpay his staff, he feels he pays the right amount, thus the work would cost €6000 in total. The Italian then enters the room. "What is there to think about, Signor Mayor?", he says, who he's known since they were kids. "My estimate is clearly the best: €3000 for me, €3000 for you, and €3000 to pay the German guy to do the work". Thus, the Italian wins the contract.

Of course, it's no laughing matter. A close friend of Stefania's was the victim of the *raccomandazioni* culture a few years ago at one of the main Universities in Italy. She had been working on short-term contracts for several years, doing research, teaching at the University, and so on. She had worked hard and had built up a very strong CV, with lots of publications, international conference presentations and so on. Finally, a *posto fisso* was advertised at the University, in exactly her field of study. Everyone in the Department told her she should get the job no problem with all of her experience. There was no one else around that could compete with her background.

Two weeks before the interviews took place, one

of the Professors in the Department called her into her office, and told her to sit down. "I'm really sorry, Daniela", she said, "but there's a *raccomandata* for this post you've applied for". Daniela's face fell to the ground and she got that awful gut-wrenching feeling to her stomach. She knew immediately what this meant. After working hard for almost 10 years for this moment, she knew fine well that there was no way she was going to win the post. She duly went along for the interview, and it turned out as she expected: someone else, from out of the blue, won the *posto fisso,* despite not having a fraction of the experience and qualifications that she had. It turns out that it was someone who was known to the Head of Department. Daniela knew that she might have to wait another 10 years for the next chance of a *posto fisso*.

You see, the "recommendation" might not always be for a family member directly. It could be that a person owes a favour to someone else, and therefore a way of returning the favour is to offer a post to the person, or a family member of that person. I remember Giorgio Napolitano - the Italian president for 9 years until he retired at the grand old age of 89 in 2015 - making a passionate speech a few years ago about the scourge of Italy. No, not the mafia or organised crime (though they perhaps have a part to play in all of this too), but he was talking about the culture of *raccomandazioni* that goes on in all walks of Italian life: in both the public and the private sector. As he highlighted in his speech, the practice continues despite widespread recognition by most Italians that it should be discouraged and eventually wiped out. He argued that if Italy continues to embrace this way of dishing out jobs, they will always be held back in their endeavours to become one of the world's top economic superpowers. Since, if there are people doing all kinds of jobs who are not amongst the most highly skilled and competent to do these jobs, clearly the economy will suffer. As well as other risks that such a culture might entail: for example, lives lost when they would otherwise be avoided, children not being educated in the best way possible, roads being built with major structural problems, and so on, and so forth.

Stefania has always likened it to sharing out a big pizza. The pizza has to be divided up in order to feed several thousands (or millions) of people. You're starving, and you really want a slice. You know that the way they're sharing it out is all wrong. There will be some that will not get any pizza at all, but you know that you're guaranteed a small slice that will keep you ticking over for a little while. However, you know for sure that there are others who are getting a much bigger slice than you are. What do you do? Do you stick your head up above the parapet and demand that the pizza is shared more fairly, thus risking that you get any pizza at all, or certainly less than you're getting at the moment? Or do you keep quiet and go along with the pizza sharing system, in the full knowledge that it's wrong and unfair, but at least you're getting a tiny slice out of it? Unfortunately, it seems - for the time being, anyway - most Italians go for the latter option. And it would take several hundred thousand of Italians with enough guts to get together to try to challenge the system. It might happen in another generation or two. Or it might not. A lot of Italians feel that the only way to get around the system is to move abroad.

Since I've been living here I've heard of - and known personally - so many people that have decided to move abroad to find work: mostly to London, or the UK, but also to many other places, such as Germany, Spain and France. The problem is that there are fewer and fewer opportunities on the island, and for the few jobs that are available, the culture of *raccomandazioni* is rife. This drives a lot of young people away as they have so little hope of being offered a good job. I wondered aloud one day at one of our family get-togethers if there was a mass exodus going on in Sardinia at the moment. However, my father-in-law explained to me that emigration has been an issue for Sardinians for decades. In fact, as long as he has been alive.

After the Second World War, it was common for Sardinians (he claims tens of thousands though he was unable to offer any official government statistics on the matter) to emigrate from the island in the 1950s and 1960s, some to the "peninsula" (this is what the Sardinians call the Italian mainland), but many others, probably more, to Germany. Sardinia seems to have a closer connection with Germany than any other part of Europe. Many of these emigrants came back to Sardinia after staying in Germany for 10 or 20 years, sometimes with German partners and families, and of course others have stayed in Germany, meaning that there is much coming and going between the two places.

One of Stefania's older cousins, Patrizia, is married to Gianni, one of these "*tedeschi*", who was born and raised in Germany to Sardinian parents because his father was working there at the time. The family stayed in Germany for around 20 years but moved back to Sardinia in the late 1970s when Gianni was 18 years old. Gianni, as you might expect, speaks fluent German and also speaks the Sardinian dialect, as they live in San Vito (Sardinian is spoken in the more rural parts of Sardinia). Italian is his third language, which can make our conversations a little difficult at times. Gianni's older brother stayed in Germany and is married to a German woman, and they now have two grown up German children. They visit Sardinia every summer, alongside tens of thousands of other German tourists - they almost outnumber the locals during the peak time in August. Many of these "tourists" are actually relatives of the locals with strong Sardinian roots who are staying with family in the area.

A further twist to the German connection to this

side of Stefania's family is that Patrizia and Gianni's daughter, Alessia, who is now in her early 30s, is married to another "*tedeschi*", also called Gianni. Young Gianni was also born and raised in Germany to Sardinian parents, but moved back here in the late 1980s when he was 14 years old. Young Gianni speaks Italian perfectly (as well as other languages) but insists, perhaps understandably when I grilled him on the matter, that his mother-tongue is German. Even if he considers himself more Sardinian than German.

A couple of years after we moved to Sardinia we were invited to Alessia and Young Gianni's wedding. It was my first real experience of a proper Italian wedding (that includes my own, which was, of course, only half-Scottish and half-Italian). The wedding took place in San Vito, and everything about it was just eye-opening for me. First of all, the numbers involved – more than 300 guests – but also it was full of tradition.

In the morning of the ceremony, a large group of us (not all 300 of us, but the most important ones!) had to follow Gianni to Alessia's house, where she was still living with her parents. It was a bizarre scene. About 70-100 people crowded around the front door of their house waiting for the bride to finish her hair and make-up and get her wedding dress on. With all the wedding guests looking on, Gianni had to wait at the front door as the final preparations were being made inside. Once the front door opened and out she came, there was cheering, and yelling and rice thrown, as well as some crockery thrown to the ground (the tradition has it that the broken plates should be shattered into as many pieces as possible as this is a sign of the bride's fertility). Then we had to all follow the bride and groom as they led the way to the church for the ceremony. It was like that scene from the Godfather with Al Pacino and Simonetta Stefanelli in Sicily.

The reception was a grand affair. The wedding party hired out an entire restaurant to accommodate the 300 guests, overlooking the sea on a fine summer's evening. The meal was incredible. I've described elsewhere the usual elaborate meal, but the number of *antipasti, primi piatti*, and *secondo piatti*, as well as the *contorni* that were brought out to us by the waitressing staff was endless. The best way for me to describe the evening is thus: Imagine you have gone to a well-to-do and well-stocked restaurant and after looking at the menu for several minutes you fail to decide on what to order. At that point, the waiter comes over to your table and can see your anguish, so he announces that the restaurant owner has decided to bring a you a decent sized serving from everything that is on the menu: vegetarian dishes, meat dishes, fish dishes, seafood: everything that is written for each course. And imagine that in addition he says he will let you have as much fine wine as you would like: red, white, rose, and he'll even throw in a liquor and a coffee, a selection of fresh fruit, as well as a slice of wedding cake.

Well, that's how it was for us at the dad. The meal began at around 8pm and the food just kept coming and coming. It was like there was a conveyor belt of serving plates somewhere in the restaurant that just wouldn't stop. It reminded me of the Generation Game[10]. Only it kept coming. And I didn't have to remember everything in order to receive it. But there wasn't a cuddly toy. And Bruce Forsyth wasn't there. Or Larry Grayson. Or even Isla St Clair (more's the pity).

We were still sitting at the table at 2am. It was a far cry from *"just get the food down ye, so we can clear the tables and get the disco on. Then we can get on wae some real drinking"*. I've said this before but it's true: eating, and not drinking, is the focus over here (though alcohol is consumed as well, just perhaps not in as large quantities as I'm used to). Also, there was no distinction of being invited for the 'full wedding/meal' and 'evening only'. Everyone who Alessia and Young Gianni wanted at their wedding came to the whole thing. 'Evening only' invitations are just not the done thing over here. The meal lasts the whole evening, so it would be impossible to distinguish between these two 'classes' of wedding

---

[10] The Generation Game, for those of you that don't know, was a family-based programme shown on British television mainly in the 1970s and 1980s. Its feature game was at the end where contestants had to memorise as many items (or prizes) as they could that would pass them on a never-ending conveyor belt.

guests.

There were other things going on that went from the strange to the bizarre to the sublime. Firstly, there is a tradition of giving the bride and groom bread at the table in the shape of both male and female genitalia. Then there is the custom of everyone shouting out "hooh raah" every 5 minutes or so, like the All Blacks rugby team doing their Haka. Usually a small group initiates it, and everyone has to join in. Alternatively, there are the shouts of *"Bacio, bacio, bacio"* that will go on for several minutes until the groom finally succumbs to the pressure and plants one on his new wife, which is met with a massive round of applause. The *bacio* chant will be repeated at regular intervals during the evening, just to make sure you don't fall asleep. And if that doesn't work then a group of the groom's friends will suddenly appear dressed up as women, blowing horns and causing a right racket, and go around the tables looking for an offering for the newly-wed couple. On Alessia and Gianni's wedding night, this group even followed them back to their house, preventing them from going to bed, and they wouldn't stop until they gave them breakfast.

The wedding was a wonderful day and a fabulous *festa*. Truly unforgettable. I've been to quite a few weddings since, but Alessia and Gianni's just sticks in the memory. And it wasn't even finished at that point. The next day we were invited to Patrizia and Gianni's house (the bride's parents) for the post-wedding celebration for family only. Young Gianni's family cooked the *maialetto* (suckling pig) on the spit and brought it to the house on these huge wooden serving plates, about a metre in length. Patrizia and Gianni prepared everything else. We just sat all day over another long meal, reminiscing about the previous day's events. There were about 40 of us in total. Sardinians, Germans and a Scottish guy.

One thing I remember about that day was after the meal, some of the males present engaged in a rather unusual game of shouting and pointing random numbers of fingers at each other. I discovered later that it's a Sardinian pastime called "*Sa Murra*", an ancient game that's been played for centuries, and extremely bizarre to observe. It's fast paced and very difficult to keep up with. They play one-on-one for several minutes continuously shouting out numbers and pointing various numbers of fingers to each other. It looks really difficult to play, and indeed it is reserved only for the few who have learned how to do it, so it's not the most inclusive of games. There must be training camps somewhere where you can learn this kind of stuff.

The other pastime I've learned over the years after moving here is playing card games like "*scopa*" and "*briscola*", using these strange cards originally from Napoli (actually, I'm a bit confused about this as they're called "*Carte Napoletane*" but they're made in Treviso in the north-east of Italy).

They're like the traditional cards but instead of clubs, hearts, spades, and diamonds they are categorised as *denari* (coins), *coppe* (cups), *bastoni* (sticks), and *spade* (swords), and they don't have 8s, 9s, and 10s, but they do have a *fante* (foot soldier), a *cavalieri* (a knight) and a *re* (a king), so 40 cards in total rather than the usual 52. Anyway, these games are a little easier to understand than *Su Murru*, and everyone is welcome to join in. I actually prefer playing card games with these *napoletane* cards now rather than with the traditional variety. They're much more beautiful to look at, and it just constitutes another part of my cultural adaptation (or sometimes referred to as *trying my best to fit in*).

They say that those Sardinians who move away from the island for work, or for other reasons, always come back to live at some point. That was certainly the case for Gianni and Young Gianni. It may take them 5 years, or 5 decades, to realise what they're missing, but they always come back. Maybe that's not true in all cases, but in my experience of meeting people over here, it certainly does seem to be common. Of course, in my own personal situation, it is also true. So, what is it all about? Do they just get so homesick that they feel there's no alternative other than moving back? But is that not true for everyone who moves to a different country to live? Is it true for me? How do I feel about living in Sardinia? About *being Scottish in Italy*? As I looked out towards the sea and the moonlit sky at Alessia and Gianni's wedding, just over 2 years had passed since I had moved here from Scotland. I started to reflect on all of this. This is what I came up with.

CHAPTER THIRTY-TWO

Being *scozzese* in Italy

Before I moved to Sardinia several people kept telling me that it might take a while for me to settle and feel at home in a new place. Especially given that I was moving to a culture that was considered so far removed from my own. At the beginning of this book I recalled the advice given to me by my boss Jim - that I should "give it at least 2 years" to see how I felt. Any less, he said, and I would not be giving the move enough time for me to feel settled. He recalled the story of his cousin, Jean, who moved to Canada when she was roughly the same age as I was when I moved. Slightly reluctant and unsure about the move, Jean apparently said to Jim that she would give it at least a couple of years but, after which, she'd probably then move back to Scotland. 40 years on and she was still in Canada, with little likelihood of moving back to her 'homeland'. I promised myself that I'd "give it 2 years" before I decided how I felt about the move. By the time I was reflecting on this at Alessia and Gianni's wedding, I had been living in Sardinia for just over two years.

I remember reading somewhere of the process that one goes through when moving to a new culture. When you arrive, you experience what is familiarly known as *culture shock*. But then you go through a *honeymoon phase*, or sometimes referred to as a *tourist phase*. This is the first few weeks where you are enthusiastic about the move and your new environment. The differences between your own culture and where you're living now might be stimulating and exciting.

After a month or two, all the excitement from the first few weeks begins to fade away and will be replaced by a level of frustration and perhaps even anger. This is known as the *negotiation phase*, or *the irritation-to-anger phase*. The differences between your home and the new environment become more obvious and may not all be welcomed. However, after these feelings of frustration and alienation pass, the emigrant should move into a new phase of *adjustment*, which could take as much as six-to-twelve months to reach. In this phase, things are no longer new and shocking all the time, and you have come to know what to expect from the new place you are in. You begin to accept the new culture, and accept that you are now living in another environment.

The final stage is the *adoption stage*, where you even begin to take on certain customs of the culture that you're living in. You might not completely renounce your own culture, although some people will do. You may even decide to apply for full citizenship of your new country. At this point, you may suffer *reverse culture shock* if you were to move back to your country of origin.

After just over two years, where was I on this scale?

I think it's fair to say that I was definitely at the adoption stage, and I still am. And I get asked all the time, both over here and when I'm back in Scotland: which country do I prefer? Is life better in Sardinia or in Scotland?

It's not an easy question to answer, and while it may seem like I'm copping out when I say, "*there are pros and cons to both*", it's just the truth. By living over here, you have to accept the whole package: the good and the bad. I am constantly annoyed by the endless bureaucracy, the fact that I have to give up whole mornings to execute a simple transaction at the bank or if I need to go to the post office or attend a medical appointment. I hate the existence of *zanzare, raccomandazioni* and *graffiti*, the lack of economic growth and infrastructure, the shortage of job opportunities, the dangerous driving, the lack of queuing, the poor-quality tea, and the fact that I have to pay more than 2 Euros for a tin of baked beans.

But I'm still happy to put up with these things. Why? Well, the one major thing that living over here offers me is a climate that is incomparable to anything I have ever had in my life in Scotland. It's November now and I'm sitting in my terrace with my shorts and t-shirt and sandals, and the hot sun is pleasantly warming me as I type. I haven't worn socks for 6 months (well, it cuts down on the washing and the lazy side of me likes the fact that I don't have to put them on in the morning).

But a climate like this offers so much more than "sunny days" and "no socks for 6 months". The warm climate affects your mood, your ability to go out and about, your diet (as long as you stay away from the bars every morning), and you can enjoy pleasures such as going down to the beach at 7pm on a weekday evening for a quick swim, or first thing in the morning (and feel like you're *Montalbano*).

You can eat out on the terrace for every meal - breakfast, lunch and dinner - for around 8 months of the year. Now that's something that you can't enjoy everywhere. And while these things might not be everybody's cup of tea, it is mine. Even if you do have to remember to buy in a few packets of Tetley's or Typhoo on your visits back to the UK.

Stefania always complained that, while she

enjoyed living in Scotland, and she lived there for over 10 years, the one thing that she found most difficult, and that ultimately motivated her to move back to Sardinia, was the weather. She became depressed from October to March because of the lack of sunlight (having lived with someone who suffers it, I do believe in SAD - Seasonal Affective Disorder). She couldn't cope with the fact that she was stuck in the house with the kids while it was pelting it down with rain, or when it was too windy, or too cold. She felt that it was more difficult to keep to a healthy diet as perhaps naturally, you want to eat more stodgy, heavy kinds of food when living in a colder climate, and she never felt the urge to go for an early morning swim down Portobello beach (why ever not? you may be asking ... or perhaps not).

The climate and the lifestyle suit me. I enjoy them, and as far as I am concerned, they are both completely different to the life I led in Scotland, in a positive way. I like the *cibo*. I like going to the bars, to the *panificio* for my bread, the local market for my delicious, fresh 0km fruit and vegetables, and I like going to the butchers and the fishmongers for my meat and fish. And I like that they all know my name and I know theirs. I like going to all the *festa* that we're invited to. I like going to the beach from May to October. Especially in the evenings after leaving work. I like the fact that we do a lot of things during the week, in the evenings, rather than having my social life revolving around the weekend only. I like the *sagra*, the *presepe,* the *Befana,* and all the religious stuff that goes on at Christmas and Easter time (as well as all the Saint days that give us a day off). I like the attitude of Italians towards children. I like *Carnevale*. In fact, I like a lot of other things about living here that I've either temporarily forgotten about or they haven't quite entered my consciousness yet. I even like the *bidet*.

However, in saying all of this, there are a lot of things I miss about living in Scotland. I miss the green. Over here the landscape is more yellow than green. It's dry and arid, and my heart weeps when we cross over a bridge of a 'river' that no longer exists because of the hot, dry climate. While the climate in Scotland might not be too auspicious, it does lead to a landscape that is one of the most beautiful in the world, especially in the Highlands, and I miss that.

I miss the banter. I miss being able to have a coffee with some milk in it, at whatever time of day I choose. I miss my family and friends. I miss being able to call up one of my mates and going round to his house to watch a football match with him that night. I miss tray bakes, scones, fudge, tablet, sliced sausage, haggis, black pudding (especially Stornoway black pudding), fish suppers, Irn Bru, steak pie, shortbread, ginger wine, and many other things, though they're probably all bad for me. I miss being in the car and switching on the radio and hearing my own language. I miss the long summer days where it doesn't get dark until 11pm or even midnight. I miss being able to go out and about at any time of the day during July and August (unless it's pelting it down with rain, of course!). And I miss not having to have four showers a day during the summer months.

I miss the more considerate driving. I miss the queuing. I miss being able to cross a road without having to put my own life at risk in the process. I miss being able to go to the doctors, or the bank, or the post office, and not having to give up my whole morning. I miss people trying their best to be punctual. I miss the simplicity of how things are done, without having to fill in endless forms and produce several documents. I miss meeting up with friends somewhere and being able to drive directly to get there, on my own, following my own route, rather than having to follow each other in convoy. I miss being able to pop out to the shops without having to remember to take some form of identification with me. I miss having to spend only 80p for a pint of fresh milk, or £2 for a packet of decent cereal. I miss seeing walls and buildings that are not completely covered in graffiti. I miss driving on a road that isn't full of pot-holes. I miss going to my bed calmly at night knowing that I won't get attacked by *zanzare*. And I miss being able to play a game of table football with people who are just as incompetent at it as I am.

Sometimes I even miss the rain for fuck's sake.

I miss a lot of things, but then, if we were to move back to Scotland, I'd miss just as many things about here. And that's the crux. There's some great things about living in both places. I suppose, without trying to sound trite, it all depends on what you make of it. Wherever you are. All things considered, I think I'm going to be ok. I think I'll hang around here for a little while more. Maybe the next 40 years or so. Then I can safely say that I have given it my best to adapt. But change my citizenship to being Italian? Let's just say I'm happy for the moment for my status to remain *Being Scottish in Italy*.

Epilogue

The vast majority of this book is based on the first two years of my life in Sardinia. All the stories you have read are true. Nothing has been invented or fabricated, though some of the reported events did occur after the first two years. As I write this Epilogue, it's now more than 9 years since we moved to Sardinia and we're still here. I haven't moved back to Scotland. Apart from the fact that I'm still enjoying the "pros" and still putting up with the "cons", I can see three other reasons why I haven't had itchy feet to move back 'home'.

The first reason relates to my close group of friends that I met two years after moving to Sardinia, and not long after I finished the first draft of my book. The *Celts in Cagliari* are a group of Scots and Irish lads, most of us married to

Sardinian women who meet up two or three times a month for a beer and a chat about what it's like to be an ex-pat living in Cagliari. We also play traditional music in a bar in Cagliari, which is now firmly established as our 'local' – Lima Lima, just off via Garibaldi. We're not a large group – three or four of us are stalwarts that are still here, others come and go depending on their respective personal situations. I owe a lot to them, in particular to Brendan, Pat, and Christy, the three mainstays of *Celts in Cagliari*. Without them I'm not sure how settled I would feel here. We support each other, laugh together, play music, relentlessly take the piss out of each other and generally hang out in a similar way as we would back home. Meeting up with the guys is an important part of my life now and, thankfully, Stefania fully understands it.

The second reason is down to the fact that I finally found a *posto fisso*. After working at the University for the first three years, and then doing *progetti* of English language work in many schools around Cagliari, in 2016 I was offered a job working in an international school in Cagliari – where I teach mathematics in English and try my best to offer my expertise (don't laugh) in bilingualism. It's a great job and I know I'm lucky to have a fixed job in Sardinia. It's been a vital peg in the puzzle of my permanence here in Sardinia. I enjoy my job and I particularly love where the school is situated – right in the heart of the

Villanova district of Cagliari.

There are four historical districts in Cagliari: Castello (the castle – the oldest part), Marina (right near the port, as the name suggests), Stampace (the more upmarket area with gorgeous villas and tree-lined avenues) and Villanova (the New town, though it is anything but new). Villanova has a wonderful atmosphere about it. It still has a village feel, much like it must have had centuries ago. Everyone seems to know each other. It is full of independently-owned shops and bars, and also little markets, artists' studios, churches and piazzas. The thing I love about this part of Cagliari, and indeed in many other cities of Italy, is that the historical buildings and roads have been maintained. They have not been bulldozed and changed into a modern, concrete monstrosity as had happened in many towns and cities in the UK. I'm afraid to say that Kilmarnock, where I am from, is a case in point. They knocked down many parts of the town in the 1970s to make way for an anonymous looking town centre and a bizarre (and to any visitors to the town - confusing) one-way system that lacks character and substance.

Anyway, back to Villanova. Every morning I walk along Via San Giovanni to get to the school, past *Pasticceria Manuel* (it has been alleged that I stop there each morning for a freshly made *bomba alla crema* – outrageous claims), and after a pleasant 10-minute walk I find myself in via San Giacomo, where the school is situated. The school is very close to Piazza San Domenico, a beautiful little piazza that has three or four bars and restaurants. The bars and restaurants fill up with the locals at night-time, especially during the summer months. It's lively, vibrant and worth a visit if you are ever in Cagliari. The piazza is even sometimes the venue for open-air concerts. Those of us who work at the school sometimes go there at lunchtime for a bite to eat and a bit of relaxation time before being set upon again in the afternoon. It's so wonderfully quiet at that time of the day compared to the evenings. Spending time in the piazza and just walking through the streets of Villanova to get to my work in the mornings is a real pleasure. I just love it. And I can't imagine having as pleasant a walk to get to work back in Scotland.

Finally, the third reason why I'm still in Sardinia is the growing appreciation of the wonderful island in which I now live my life. After several years of talking about it, last year we finally decided to hire a campervan for five days and explore parts of Sardinia that we hadn't visited before. It was a fantastic holiday and we took in some spectacular places that I hadn't seen before in all the time I've been living here. We went to Tempio-Pausania, a beautiful, picturesque town in the north-east of Sardinia that gives the impression of being in one of the northern regions of Italy like Trentino-Alto Adige or Veneto or Valle d'Aosta. The architecture is beautiful and the town has a lovely ambience about it. It's not so big and you can explore it at a leisurely pace in just one day.

We travelled from Tempio-Pausania up to the northern coastline to places like Castelsardo and Stintino. While I've always been fond of the southeast coast (places such as Villasimius and Costa Rei), I can see that it is only one of many gorgeous coastlines in Sardinia. Stintino is often quoted as being amongst the best beaches in the whole of the Mediterranean and you can see why. It's breathtaking. From there we drove down to Alghero. I had visited Alghero before, but it reminded me of how unique this little corner of Sardinia is. Alghero was under Spanish rule for centuries and it hasn't lost that Hispanic feel to it. Indeed, the language of the locals is an interesting mix of Italian, Spanish and Sardinian. It's difficult to understand and so I just stick to Italian when I'm there. From there we drove down the coastline (again spectacular) to truly one of the most enchanting places I've ever been. The small town of Bosa, which is about 45 kilometres from Alghero, stole my heart after spending just 24 hours traipsing its streets and peering in on its ancient houses. I'm not going to try to describe Bosa. I know I'll fail to capture its unique beauty. I urge you to take a visit. It was shortlisted a few years ago for the award of *"il borgo dei borghi d'Italia"* (the most beautiful village in Italy). Finally, the last stop on our whistle-stop tour was S'Archittu, a naturally formed arch that crosses the sea on the coastline towards Oristano. People dive off from the arch into the water. I didn't quite have the courage to do it myself, but I enjoyed watching others do it.

It was a marvellous holiday and a reminder of how lucky I am to be living in this beautiful island. And the thing is, I am 100% sure that there are many wonderful places in Sardinia that I have not mentioned in my five-day trip around the island, or indeed in the whole of this book. There is still much to discover. I'll need to hang around for a bit yet so that I can explore further this unique, picturesque and diverse island. And with Brexit around the corner, I may even decide to change my status: maybe I'll just have to get used to *Being Italian in Italy*.

ABOUT THE AUTHOR

Fraser Lauchlan is a psychologist, teacher, and researcher who has a long-standing publishing record including several books, book chapters and articles published in academic journals. He works as a mathematics teacher in a bilingual school in Cagliari, is an Honorary Lecturer at the Universities of Strathclyde (Glasgow) and Manchester, and also runs a training and consultancy business in the UK, where he provides training to teachers and educational psychologists. His web-site is www.fraserlauchlan.com . 'Being Scottish in Italy' is his first venture in mainstream writing. If you enjoyed reading this, please spread the word and write a nice review. It will be very much appreciated!

☺

Printed in Great Britain
by Amazon